The Social Studies Helper

Creative Assignments
for Exam Success

DENISE FAWCETT FACEY

ROWMAN & LITTLEFIELD EDUCATION
A division of
ROWMAN & LITTLEFIELD PUBLISHERS, INC.
Lanham • New York • Toronto • Plymouth, UK

Published by Rowman & Littlefield Education
A division of Rowman & Littlefield Publishers, Inc.
A wholly owned subsidiary of The Rowman & Littlefield Publishing Group, Inc.
4501 Forbes Boulevard, Suite 200, Lanham, Maryland 20706
http://www.rowmaneducation.com

Estover Road, Plymouth PL6 7PY, United Kingdom

British Library Cataloguing in Publication Information Available

Library of Congress Cataloging-in-Publication Data

Facey, Denise Fawcett, 1958–
  The social studies helper : creative assignments for exam success / Denise Fawcett Facey.
    p. cm.
  ISBN 978-1-60709-750-1 (cloth : alk. paper) — ISBN 978-1-60709-751-8 (pbk. : alk. paper) — ISBN 978-1-60709-752-5 (electronic)
  1. Social sciences—Study and teaching (Secondary)—Activity programs—United States. I. Title.
  H62.5.U5F33 2010
    300.71'2—dc22   2010005115

∞ ™ The paper used in this publication meets the minimum requirements of American National Standard for Information Sciences—Permanence of Paper for Printed Library Materials, ANSI/NISO Z39.48-1992.

Printed in the United States of America

Contents

Introduction

It's that time again. Classes are about to begin, and like teachers everywhere, you're setting up your classroom and preparing for the upcoming year. You really want to make this the best school year possible. But, by the time you get the bulletin boards done, the posters and banners hung, and the first week's lesson plans written—in between attending meetings—the students have arrived. Then you're teaching lessons and trying to find enough time in the day to correct homework, read essays, grade tests, and do all of those other things that go with teaching.

Whether you are a novice or a veteran teacher, on a traditional schedule of forty-five or fifty-five minutes per class period or a block schedule with ninety minutes, there's little time left to come up with innovative activities and projects. Yet these make such an important difference in the classroom. Creative assignments can enhance your lessons, spark student interest, and serve as an assessment of genuine learning that tests do not always measure. That's where this book can help.

Busy teachers and those just seeking new ideas can use *The Social Studies Helper* as a resource throughout the school year. Now you have activities and projects instantly available and ready for use, without having to set aside the time to develop them. Creating projects and activities need no longer be on your "to do" list!

Designed to augment students' test-taking skills and abilities, the assignments offered here have been successfully tested on high school students with various learning styles, in regular and gifted classes. Each of the traditionally required social studies courses—from world geography to economics—is covered in separate chapters that easily integrate technology and content. A couple of chapters on elective courses are also in the book.

For the purposes of this book, we distinguish between *projects* and *activities*. Projects are long-term assignments, taking about a month to complete. These projects require that students conduct research outside of the class period, either independently or in small groups. In contrast, the activities are in-class assignments that the students can complete in one or two periods, usually working in small groups.

Each assignment has an overview, fully describing the assignment and providing step-by-step procedures for the teacher. Within that overview, each assignment is labeled to indicate whether it is a motivating activity or project designed to begin a lesson or unit, a building activity or project to link concepts, or a culminating activity or project that enables you to assess learning outcomes. Also, since some of the assignments are intended for independent effort and others for group work, this is noted at the beginning of each activity or project.

For the projects, a handout for the students follows each overview. These handouts provide specific guidelines for the research papers that many of these projects require and explain all other requirements for completing the project. And since you need a fair and equitable method for grading these projects, immediately following each handout is a corresponding rubric.

The handouts and rubrics are ready for use or may serve as templates for designing your own documents. Each of these documents contains blanks to allow the teacher to set standardized guidelines for formatting the research papers.

This brings us to technology. Since we live in a global society that increasingly relies on technology, students in our twenty-first-century classrooms need to be adept at using it. With this in mind, the projects and many of the activities offered here involve the Internet as a resource. Students are already familiar with the Internet through their frequent use of social websites and music downloads, so it's easy for them to navigate the web as they work on these assignments. Search engines such as Google are particularly helpful in locating pertinent websites. And if the teacher restricts the students' Internet research to scholarly websites and mandates that they correctly cite these sources in their research papers, the students' efforts on these assignments can simultaneously build their skills and prepare them for future college coursework.

In cognitive terms, the assignments are at the upper levels of Bloom's taxonomy. This compels students to use higher-order thinking skills: analysis, synthesis, and evaluation. Additionally, all of the activities and projects address visual, auditory, and kinesthetic learning styles and have objectives indicated in behavioral terms. These objectives allow you to see at a glance what skills and concepts your students are gaining.

Finally, although many of the assignments are accessible to all types of learners, differentiating assignments by ability level can sometimes be helpful. That's why this book offers tips for differentiation, as needed, with a particular emphasis on modifications for special education students who have processing difficulties.

Simply use the projects and activities in the same manner in which they are presented or rework them in whatever way is best for you. For instance, in addition to differentiating these assignments by ability level, as suggested, you may want to adapt some of the projects to another course. The Family Heritage Project in the world geography chapter, for example, can be assigned in a world history or U.S. history course, with minor changes.

Everything about this book is meant to take some of the pressure off the teacher. With one less thing to worry about, teaching just became a little bit easier! So, get a cup of coffee or tea, and sit down and discover just how easy it is to enhance your lessons.

1

World Geography

World geography is usually taught to freshmen in one semester. Given that these new high school students experience equal parts exhilaration and trepidation, ninth grade teachers often find it helpful to have assignments that meet two goals: channeling the students' exuberance and acclimating them to high school standards. Therefore, the group activities and projects in this chapter meet the first goal, and the independent assignments address the latter goal.

Freshmen benefit from group work because it requires them to act collaboratively, building such skills as prioritizing, collating, and integrating information. Plus, group work provides a social outlet. It's an opportunity for a bit more "fun" in an educational manner. This enjoyment effectively directs the students' high spirits and can curtail classroom management issues. With these things in mind, this chapter's activities and two of its projects involve group participation.

On the other hand, the independent assignments in this chapter are designed to help freshmen acquire research skills that can prepare them for advanced courses that rely on these skills. These independent assignments also give the students the autonomy to highlight their creative talents and abilities.

Of course, the main point in all of the assignments is content. That's why the five themes of geography (location, place, human and environment interaction, movement, and region) are integral to the assignments in this chapter. Including these themes reinforces the primary concepts that teachers focus on in geography. Therefore, each of the projects and activities addresses one or more themes, which is indicated on every assignment.

OVERVIEW: WORLD GEOGRAPHY ACTIVITY I—WHERE DO YOU LIVE? (MAPPING)

Activity Type: Motivating; Independent and Group

Themes: Place, Location

Materials: Internet access, paper, colored pencils or markers

Objectives: To introduce the students to the study of place and location by developing maps, students must:

1. Design a neighborhood map.
2. Develop a community map by merging the neighborhood maps.
3. Create a compass rose and a map legend.
4. Analyze their own communities.
5. Distinguish between absolute and relative location.
6. Identify longitude and latitude.
7. Appraise local culture.

Description: This activity requires two class periods. After the teacher has taught basic map skills, including the function of the compass rose and map legend, this activity can introduce the students to the concepts of place and location. Each student designs his or her own neighborhood map. Then the students combine the maps to create one large community map.

Procedure: Students draw maps of the neighborhood surrounding their homes during one class period. The maps must include the following:

1. A line drawing of the general neighborhood
2. A symbol or drawing to indicate their own homes
3. A symbol or drawing to indicate neighborhood landmarks
4. Street names
5. A compass rose
6. A legend that clearly explains the symbols used

The students combine the neighborhood maps during the second class period.

1. The students work in small groups to join their neighborhood maps.
2. Then the class merges the neighborhood maps developed by the small groups to form a community map. The community map must also include symbols or drawings of schools, fire and police stations, houses of worship, stores, and entertainment places.
3. The students use websites such as world.maporama.com or www.infoplease.com/atlas/latitude-longitude.html to determine their community's latitude and longitude. This portion of the activity allows the teacher to introduce the students to relative and absolute location.
4. The teacher then leads the class in discussing what the community map tells about the people and their culture.
5. The teacher displays the map in the classroom.

Differentiation: When gifted students create the individual neighborhood maps, they might also write and present an essay that narrates what is seen while driving through their neighborhood. Special education students might present and explain the individual neighborhood maps instead of creating the community map. The special education students might then limit the discussion portion of this activity to comparing and contrasting the neighborhoods.

OVERVIEW: WORLD GEOGRAPHY ACTIVITY II—HAPPY EARTH DAY! (ENVIRONMENTALISM)

Activity Type: Building; Group

Themes: Movement, Human and Environment Interaction

Materials: Internet access

Objectives: To develop students' understanding of human influence on the environment, students must:

1. Research environmental problems.
2. Determine which problem to solve.
3. Devise a plan for solving the environmental problem.
4. Implement the plan school-wide.
5. Publicize the solution.
6. Recommend changes that can prevent recurrence of the problem.

Description: This activity is ongoing throughout the school year. The students must develop a plan to solve a specific environmental problem that they then research. Then the students execute the plan school-wide, as the rest of the student body assists in this activity. Some problems that the students might address are recycling paper, disposing of plastic water bottles, and replacing toxic products.

Procedure: The students work in small groups to research their chosen environmental problems on the Internet.

1. Each group presents a brief description of the environmental problem that they researched.
2. The students vote on which problem is most solvable.
3. The students plan a solution that can be implemented by the entire student body.
4. The students create a method to publicize the problem and the proposed solution throughout the school.
5. The students are the leaders in putting the plan into action school-wide.
6. A student committee meets with school administrators to discuss the students' recommendations for preventing the problem from recurring.

Differentiation: This activity does not need differentiation as students undertake responsibilities according to their capabilities.

OVERVIEW: WORLD GEOGRAPHY ACTIVITY III—FOOD DAY (CULTURE'S IMPACT ON FOOD)

Activity Type: Culminating; Independent and Group

Themes: Region, Human and Environment Interaction, Movement

Materials: Internet access, food items, and paper goods

Objectives: To apply students' knowledge of place, movement, and human and environment interaction to a specific country, students must:

1. Research the climate, economy, crops, culture, and traditional foods of one country.
2. Analyze how climate, culture, and the economy influence the crops and foods in that country.
3. Collate the information into a brief paper.
4. Collaborate in creating and preparing a menu of traditional foods.

Description: This activity may be repeated at the end of every unit. It builds on students' prior knowledge of a continent. Suitable for auditory, visual, and kinesthetic learners, the activity enables students to understand how climate, crops, economy, and culture affect food traditions. In addition, students may note the similarities and differences among the various countries on that continent.

Procedure: The students work in small groups to do the majority of this activity in class. The teacher assigns each group a country from the continent that is being studied.

1. Each group uses the Internet to research the assigned country.
2. The students obtain information on the assigned country's climate, crops, culture, economy, and traditional foods.
3. Each group organizes the information that they researched into a paper to be presented in class.
4. The members of each group work together to formulate a menu of traditional foods that they then serve in class.
5. Each member of the group prepares one dish on the menu.
6. The groups present the papers and serve the foods in class.
7. The teacher leads a discussion of the similarities and differences among the continent's countries.

Differentiation: Regular education students and special education students may be assigned to research fewer factors for each country. In addition, special education students might work together to create one dish per group rather than each member of the group preparing individual dishes.

OVERVIEW: WORLD GEOGRAPHY ACTIVITY IV—WHAT'S NEW? (CURRENT EVENTS)

Activity Type: Building; Independent

Themes: Depending on the article chosen, all five themes of geography may be covered in this assignment.

Materials: Internet access

Objectives: To demonstrate the link between the concepts learned in class and events occurring in the world, students must:

1. Navigate the Internet.
2. Summarize a significant event.
3. Determine which themes of geography are represented.
4. Explain how each theme is represented.
5. Identify terms/concepts in the article that were also learned in class.
6. Express an opinion.
7. Discuss the events and opinions.
8. Critique other students' opinions.
9. Defend their own views with factual information.

Description: This assignment is designed to be recurrent throughout the semester. It requires students to research, interpret and summarize news events.

Procedure: The teacher directs the students to use the Internet for research. Students use websites such as www .nytimes.com, www.cnn.com, www.foxnews.com, or www.msnbc.msn.com to select a significant news article from the "world" or "international" sections of the website. For the purposes of this assignment, "significant" is defined as an article that is focused on an event that has high impact on a particular country or region, or has potential impact on the world. The students must write an essay with a minimum of three paragraphs. The essay must contain:

1. A summary of the event in his or her own words.
2. The specific themes of geography that are represented by the event, with details to support the selection of these themes.
3. Terms or concepts that were learned in class and are used in the article.
4. The student's opinion of the event. The opinion must be based upon facts presented in the article combined with facts learned in class.

Each student must choose a partner with whom to read and discuss the essays in class. Each member of the pair briefly explains the other student's event and the themes of geography in that event to the class. The rest of the class then offers their opinions of the event. In addition, the students challenge the opinions of others, while defending their own views with facts.

Differentiation: The teacher may assign this activity as homework for gifted and regular education classes. The students then do the reading and discussion portions of the activity in class on the day that the essay is due. The teacher might also require gifted students to include a discussion of the event's geographical significance in their essays. For special education classes, it may be beneficial to do the entire assignment in class (if a computer lab is available) so that the teacher may provide additional support.

OVERVIEW: WORLD GEOGRAPHY PROJECT I—THE UNITED STATES AND . . . OH, CANADA (LANDFORMS AND WATER FEATURES OF THE UNITED STATES AND CANADA)

Project Type: Culminating, Independent

Themes: Place, Location (absolute and relative), Human and Environment Interaction

Objectives: To demonstrate knowledge of U.S. and Canadian physical geography, students must:

1. Research the physical geography, cultures, and economies of the United States and Canada.
2. Analyze maps of both countries.
3. Identify major landforms and water features.
4. Compare and contrast the landforms and water features of the two countries.
5. Evaluate the impact of these landforms and water features on the culture(s) of the people of the region.
6. Analyze the influence of landforms and water features on both countries' economies.

Description: This project provides a broad overview of the United States and Canada's physical geography, requiring the students to note the two countries' commonalities as well as their distinguishing features. The project may focus solely on landforms or water features, or a combination of the two.

Procedure: Each student has a month to research and type a two-page paper about U.S. and Canadian landforms and water features. The paper must incorporate all of the objectives that are listed in this activity. Students must also create a visual representation of one landform or water feature. The paper and the visual representation must be presented in class.

Differentiation: The teacher may require that gifted classes research both the water features *and* the landforms. For regular education classes, the teacher might expect that students research the landforms *or* the water features, rather than both. Students in special education classes may each be assigned one specific water feature or landform. Also, for regular or special education classes you may wish to omit one or more of the objectives.

HANDOUT: WORLD GEOGRAPHY PROJECT I—THE UNITED STATES AND . . . OH, CANADA

You must research the major landforms (mountains, hills, plateaus, plains) and water features (oceans, rivers, seas, gulfs, bays, streams, lakes) on or surrounding the United States and Canada. You must:

1. Write a _____-page research paper. The paper must be _____-spaced, font size ____ and font type _____. You must include internal documentation, a complete and accurate works cited page, and a cover page.
2. Identify the major landforms and water features.
3. Compare and contrast the U.S. and Canadian landforms and water features.
4. Evaluate how these landforms and water features affect the culture of the people near the landform or water feature.
5. Analyze how these landforms and water features contribute to the formation of the two countries' economies.
6. Create an original visual representation (three-dimensional replica, poster, or other art form) of one water feature or landform. Creativity counts!

The entire project must be presented in class.

RUBRIC: WORLD GEOGRAPHY PROJECT I—THE UNITED STATES AND . . . OH, CANADA

Name _____

Grade _____

1. Research paper's format (25 points)_____
    A. Paper is at least _____ pages, _____-spaced (5 points)_____
    B. Font is size _____, type_____(5 points)_____
    C. Includes cover page (5 points) _____
    D. Internal documentation is complete and accurate (5 points) _____
    E. Works cited page is complete and accurate (5 points) _____
2. Research paper's content (40 points) _____
    A. Includes all landforms and water features (10 points) _____
    B. Has comparison *and* contrast of U.S. and Canadian landforms and water features (10 points)_____
        _____
    C. Has full evaluation of the cultural impact of these landforms and water features (10 points)_____
        _____
    D. Analyzes landforms' contributions to both countries' economies (10 points) _____
3. Visual or audio (20 points)_____
    A. Is correctly representative of the landform or water feature (10 points) _____
    B. Shows effort and creativity (10 points)_____
4. Presentation (15 points)_____
    A. Speaks clearly and with interest (5 points)_____
    B. Shows knowledge of the content (10 points)_____

OVERVIEW: WORLD GEOGRAPHY PROJECT II—IT'S VACATION TIME (LATIN AMERICA)

Project Type: Building; Independent

Themes: Place, Human and Environment Interaction, Movement, Region

Objectives: To develop knowledge of Latin America's physical and cultural geography, students must:

1. Explain the five themes of geography as they are represented in the chosen Latin American countries.
2. Describe the physical geography.
3. Analyze the countries' cultural aspects.
4. Synthesize the above information into a travel brochure or travelogue.

Description: The project's main emphasis is Latin America's physical and cultural geography. Focusing on one country at a time allows each student to become an "expert" on that country, while educating all of the students about the entire region through the presentations.

Procedure: Students choose a Latin American country and create an original travel brochure or travelogue about it. In addition to the geographical content, students must make the project visually stimulating, highlighting the major points of interest in their chosen country, so as to entice tourists to visit.

The brochure or travelogue must:

1. Explain how the five themes of geography are displayed in that country.
2. Describe the country's physical geography.
3. Highlight the country's cultural aspects, including language, religion, values, and currency, among other factors.
4. By giving the students the choice between a brochure (a written project) and a travelogue (a project that combines the visual and the auditory), the students can work in the style that is most conducive to their own personal learning.

Differentiation: Teachers of gifted classes might direct the students to create a television commercial or radio advertisement to accompany the brochure, which is essentially a synthesis of the two options presented for the project. For special education classes, teachers may prefer to amend the third objective by specifically indicating a limited number of cultural aspects to be researched.

HANDOUT: WORLD GEOGRAPHY PROJECT II—IT'S VACATION TIME

Select any country in Latin America (Mexico, Central America, South America, or the Caribbean). Design an original travel brochure or travelogue (video or DVD) that encourages tourism. You must:

1. Fully explain the five themes of geography as they are represented in your chosen country.
2. Describe the country's physical geography.
3. Highlight the country's culture (including values, religions, language, currency).
4. Emphasize the country's major points of interest.
5. Create original visual images (drawings, photos, three-dimensional reproductions). Creativity counts!
6. Present your project in class.

RUBRIC: WORLD GEOGRAPHY PROJECT II—IT'S VACATION TIME

Name _____

Grade _____

1. The travel brochure or travelogue's content (85 points) _____
    A. Has only a Latin American country (10 points)_____
    B. Completely explains all five themes of geography as they are represented in the chosen country (20 points)____
       _____
    C. Highlights the country's culture (20 points)_____
    D. Emphasizes the major points of interest for tourists (20 points)_____
    E. Has originality and creativity (15 points)_____
2. Presentation (15 points)_____
    A. Speaks clearly (5 points)_____
    B. Shows knowledge of the content (5 points)_____
    C. Speaks with interest (5 points)_____

OVERVIEW: WORLD GEOGRAPHY PROJECT III—MY FAMILY HERITAGE (HUMAN GEOGRAPHY)

Project Type: Building and Culminating; Independent and Group

Themes: Location, Place, Human and Environment Interaction, Movement, Region

Objectives: To develop students' knowledge of the countries from which their families originate, students must:

1. Interview family members.
2. Research the countries from which their families originated.
3. Collate the information obtained from the interview and the research, and combine it in a paper.
4. Compile and interpret statistics.
5. Create a family crest.

Description: This project is designed to provide students with a personal connection to physical and cultural geography. This includes students' comprehension of the links between the original country and the United States. It also involves students' ability to collate and interpret the findings. Teachers can assign the project when the students study the continent from which the majority of the students have ancestry.

Procedure: Three products arise from this assignment: a paper, a family crest, and a graph. The first two are independent undertakings and the last is a group endeavor. Together, the three parts of the project demonstrate the countries' interdependence, the commonalities and distinctions among countries, and the students' personal links to other parts of the world.

1. Students interview their oldest relatives to obtain information about the countries from which they originated, the reasons for their immigration to the United States, their experiences upon arrival, and the difference between life in the original countries and life in the United States.
2. The students then analyze, evaluate, and synthesize the information to develop an essay.
3. Next, each student creates a family crest that includes a family motto, a family symbol or emblem, and an additional feature that links the original country to the United States. Photos or other illustrations should be included.
4. Each student must present the paper and the crest in class.
5. As each student presents, another student lists on the board all the countries represented in the class.
6. After the students complete the presentations, they work in small groups to construct a graph representing all the countries.
7. These graphs are then displayed in the classroom along with the family crests.

Differentiation: The modifications for this project are not focused on ability level, but rather on adapting the content to other courses. For a world history course, the teacher might instruct the students to research the major events taking place in the original countries and in the United States at the time of their ancestors' arrival and include these in the paper. For a U.S. history course, the teacher might require that the students research the following: the major events taking place in the United States at the time, the port of entry of their ancestors (Ellis Island or Angel Island), the location of their ancestors' settlement within the United States and the impact upon the region, and the contributions to U.S. history and culture brought by people of this (these) particular ethnic group(s).

HANDOUT: WORLD GEOGRAPHY PROJECT III—MY FAMILY HERITAGE

This project gives you the opportunity to learn about and celebrate your family heritage. It requires interviewing, research, writing, and graphing.

1. Interview your oldest available family members and find out:
   A. The countries your family came from
   B. When, why, and how your first family members came to the United States
   C. The positive and negative experiences your family members had after arrival in the United States
   D. The family traditions that have been passed down through the generations and whether they began in another country
   E. How life in the United States differs from life in the original country
2. Type a _____-page paper (_____-spaced, font size _____, font type _____). The paper must include the above information as well as any other information that makes your family unique or that you wish to share about your family.
3. Create a "family crest" that includes a family motto, a family symbol or emblem, and an additional feature that links the original country to the United States. Photos and other illustrations may be added.
4. Present both the paper and the family crest in class.
5. We list all of the countries represented by the class members as each paper is presented in class.
6. After all projects have been presented, we work in small groups to graph the listed countries.
7. We display the graphs and family crests in the classroom.

RUBRIC: WORLD GEOGRAPHY PROJECT III—MY FAMILY HERITAGE

Name_____

Grade_____

1. Paper's format (25 points)_____
   A. Paper is at least _____ pages, _____-spaced (5 points)_____
   B. Font is size _____ and font type is _____ (5 points)_____
   C. Includes cover page (5 points)_____
   D. Internal documentation is complete and accurate (5 points)_____
   E. Works cited page is complete and accurate (5 points)_____
2. Paper's content (45 points)_____
   A. Interview indicates when, why, and how family came to United States (10 points)_____
   B. Has family's positive and negative experiences on arrival in United States (10 points) _____
   C. Includes family traditions (10 points) _____
   D. Includes difference between life in original country and U.S. life (15 points)_____
3. Family crest (15 points)_____
   A. Includes family motto (5 points) _____
   B. Includes family symbol or emblem (5 points) _____
   C. Additional link between original country and United States (5 points)_____
4. Presentation (15 points)_____
   A. Speaks clearly (5 points) _____
   B. Shows knowledge of the content (5 points) _____
   C. Shows enthusiasm (5 points)_____

OVERVIEW: WORLD GEOGRAPHY PROJECT IV—THIS IS AUSTRALIA (PHYSICAL AND HUMAN GEOGRAPHY)

Project Type: Building and Culminating; Group

Themes: Location, Place, Human and Environment Interaction, Movement, Region

Objectives: To expand and assess students' basic knowledge of Australia through research, application, analysis, synthesis, and evaluation, students must:

1. Research Australia's physical geography, culture, government, and outback and cities.
2. Collaborate in groups to combine the information into one research paper per group.
3. Generate visual and/or audio representation of the research.
4. Formulate lessons and present them in class.
5. Evaluate each group member's work and contribution to the group.

Description: This project puts the students in the role of teacher. It is constructed to provide "layers" of knowledge. First, each *student* gains in-depth knowledge about a specific concept. Then, each *group* develops detailed knowledge about the topic that is researched by the group. And finally, the entire *class* acquires broad knowledge about Australia through the lessons that the students teach.

Procedure: Students work in four groups: physical geography, culture, government, and outback and cities. The teacher may randomly assign the students to groups or allow the students to choose. The students use two handouts: one that provides an overview of the entire project and another that lists the specific concepts to be researched by that group. Within each group, the students must:

1. Delegate the various concepts to be researched.
2. Collate the information to create one research paper per group.
3. Create visual or audio representations of the concepts.
4. Teach the class, using the research paper, as the rest of the students take notes.
5. Illustrate the lessons with the visual and audio representations.
6. Complete a group self-assessment form that requires each student to evaluate his or her contributions to the project as well as the contributions made by the group's other members.

Differentiation: Teachers may expect gifted classes to produce more in-depth information. These students might then write a follow-up essay (in class or for homework) in which they explain the connections among several concepts that each group presented. The students would have to justify and support their opinions by using factual information that they gained via the research. Teachers of regular education classes might require the students to have small group discussions instead of writing the essay. In special education classes, the teacher might facilitate a discussion with the entire class.

HANDOUT: WORLD GEOGRAPHY PROJECT IV—THIS IS AUSTRALIA

This project requires you to become the "teacher." You must work in four groups to research Australia's physical geography, culture, government, and outback and cities. You must use the research that you obtain to "teach" the class about Australia. In this project:

1. Each group must research a different aspect of Australia.
2. Each person has the responsibility to research one concept within that topic.
3. Each group must collate the information into one report. The report must be a minimum of _____ pages, _____-spaced. The font must be size _____ and the font type must be _____. Remember to include internal documentation, a cover page and a works cited page.
4. The group must create appropriate visuals that correspond with the concepts that the group researches.
5. The group then presents the paper and visual in class as a "lesson."
6. The class must take notes on the information presented by each group.
7. Each student must also complete and submit a group self-assessment form in class.

RUBRIC: WORLD GEOGRAPHY PROJECT IV—THIS IS AUSTRALIA

Name _____

Grade _____

1. Self-assessment grade (15 points)_____
2. The research paper's format (25 points)_____
    A. Paper is at least _____ pages, _____-spaced (5 points)_____
    B. Font size is _____ and font type is _____(5 points)_____
    C. Includes cover page (5 points)_____
    D. Internal documentation is complete and accurate (5 points)_____
    E. Works cited page is complete and accurate (5 points)_____
3. The research paper's content (30 points)_____
    A. All of the assigned concepts are researched (10 points)_____
    B. All information is collated into a cohesive paper (10 points)_____
    C. All of the information is relevant to the assigned topic (10 points)_____
4. Visual or audio (15 points)_____
    A. Is correctly representative of the assigned concept (10 points)_____
    B. Shows effort and creativity (5 points)_____
5. Presentation (15 points)_____
    A. Speaks clearly (5 points)_____
    B. Shows knowledge of the content (5 points)_____
    C. Speaks with interest (5 points)_____

Group: Self-Assessment

Name: _____

Responsibility: _____

Grading Scale: 5=Excellent; 4=Very Good; 3=Good; 2=Fair; 1=Little Effort; 0=No Effort

Assessed By	Completed Assigned Work	Quality of Work	Participation Level	Worked with Others
1. SELF				
2.				
3.				
4.				
TOTALS				

Grade: _____

GROUP HANDOUT: WORLD GEOGRAPHY PROJECT IV—THIS IS AUSTRALIA

Group One: Physical Geography

Animals

Climate and time

Landforms

Map

GROUP HANDOUT: WORLD GEOGRAPHY PROJECT IV—THIS IS AUSTRALIA

Group Two: Culture

Aborigines

Food

Language

Music

Religion

Values

GROUP HANDOUT: WORLD GEOGRAPHY PROJECT IV—THIS IS AUSTRALIA

Group Three: Government

Kind of government (head of state; head of government; branches of government)

History (formation of the country; major events)

Flag

Anthem

GROUP HANDOUT: WORLD GEOGRAPHY PROJECT IV—THIS IS AUSTRALIA

Group Four: Cities and Outback

Compare and contrast the two regions

Economy

Five themes of geography

Major points of interest

Populations

2

World History

World history is a year-long course that sophomores are usually required to take. Because spanning prehistoric times to the present in the space of one academic year is virtually impossible, teachers really need to be selective in determining which topics to skim through and which to teach on a deeper level. The activities in this chapter are designed to assist teachers in developing those more in-depth studies. An example is activity II, which compels the students to delve into Chinese belief systems as they devise fictitious civilizations based on those beliefs.

This emphasis on concentrated study also extends to the projects. Since these are culminating projects intended for the end of a unit, each project covers many concepts within one topic. Additionally, the students apply and synthesize their knowledge about these concepts as they develop the visual or audio parts of their presentations. Project I, for instance, encompasses an ancient civilization's history, culture, and traditions. The students must represent these concepts in a research paper on culture and tradition, a timeline of the historic events, and audios or visuals that combine all of the concepts.

As you look over the assignments in this chapter, you may notice that there is one activity in common with chapter 1: current events. The distinction between the two current events assignments is that each highlights different aspects of world events. For the world history course, the students focus their current events essays on the events' worldwide impact, along with their own analysis of that impact in a historical context. As a result, even students who may have done current events assignments in your world geography class approach it differently when writing about current events in your world history class.

The activities and projects in this chapter place an even greater emphasis on the three highest levels of Bloom's taxonomy. The priority is to enable students to make connections between history and the present, thereby making history more personal and more relevant to them. The cognitive direction toward analysis, synthesis, and evaluation becomes the bridge for making those connections.

OVERVIEW: WORLD HISTORY ACTIVITY I—IT'S BARTER DAY! (TRADE)

Activity Type: Motivating; Group

Objectives: To introduce students to bartering and to analyze the concept, students must:

1. Collect items from home that they wish to trade.
2. Exhibit the items in a classroom bazaar.
3. Scrutinize the items to determine the ones for which they wish to bargain.
4. Appraise the items' values.
5. Negotiate with each other to obtain the desired items.
6. Discuss their methodology for determining the items' values.
7. Compare and contrast bartering and selling.

Materials: Items that students wish to barter, a table, construction paper and/or crepe paper and/or cloth

Description: This activity is constructed to last for one class period. It is a kinesthetic learning activity that permits students to experience bartering and trade.

Procedure: The teacher directs students in advance to bring in any items they wish to use for trade on a specific day referred to as "Barter Day." On Barter Day, the items are displayed on a table that the students have decorated with construction paper or crepe paper.

1. Students peruse the tables before bartering begins to determine what they wish to obtain.
2. Students then determine what they are willing to trade to obtain the desired items.
3. Bartering begins with the "traders" determining what they want in exchange for the items presented for barter.
4. The "customers" decide what they are willing to trade in return.
5. This bartering continues until all items are traded or until there are none left for which anyone wishes to barter.
6. The teacher conducts a class discussion on the experience. This includes discussing the students' methods of determining the bartered items' value as well as a comparison and contrasting of bartering versus selling.
7. The teacher then teaches a lesson about bartering in ancient civilizations.

Differentiation: For gifted classes, the teacher may require that students design a follow-up activity in which they barter for services rather than goods. The students may decide to continue offering those services throughout the school year.

OVERVIEW: WORLD HISTORY ACTIVITY II—MY THEOCRACY'S BETTER THAN YOURS! (CHINESE BELIEF SYSTEMS)

Activity Type: Building; Group

Objective: To apply students' knowledge of Chinese belief systems, students must:

1. Form groups based on their understanding of Chinese belief systems.
2. Invent a "country" whose government is founded on one Chinese belief system.
3. Formulate a basic constitution that incorporates the belief system.
4. Create a culture that stems from the country's belief system.
5. Construct consequences for violation of the constitution.

Materials: index cards, large sheets of construction paper, markers or crayons

Description: This activity, designed to take one class period, combines students' existing knowledge with their creativity. Designed for kinesthetic learning, it reinforces concepts that students have already learned by having the students group themselves based on their understanding of Chinese belief systems. The activity's creative outlet is via the students' invention of countries whose government, culture, and social interactions are based upon one of the belief systems.

Procedure: The teacher writes one characteristic from each of the major ancient Chinese belief systems (Buddhism, Confucianism, Daoism, and Legalism) on separate index cards. The name of the belief should not be written on the cards. The number of characteristics needed is determined by the number of students in the class.

1. Each student is directed to choose one index card from the pile without first reading the card.
2. Using the characteristics indicated on each card, students must group themselves by belief system.
3. Each group invents a "country" based on the beliefs that are indicated on the index cards. They then represent that country in a poster.
4. The poster must contain: a name for the country, a government with a constitution and consequences based on the belief system, a culture that includes the protocols for interactions among family members and friends/neighbors.
5. The groups present and explain their "countries" to the class.
6. The class discusses the feasibility of each country's existence based on their knowledge of the belief systems. They also discuss whether these countries could coexist.

All posters are displayed in the classroom.

Differentiation: All ability levels could participate in this activity as it is designed. As a follow-up assignment, gifted classes could conduct a debate on the significance of religion's role in government. Students in regular education classes may be assigned to write an essay on their opinion of religion's role in government and discuss the essays in class. Those in special education classes might view a movie which depicts religion in a society, and then discuss their reactions to the movie.

OVERVIEW: WORLD HISTORY ACTIVITY III—WHAT'S GOING ON IN THE WORLD? (CURRENT EVENTS)

Activity Type: Building; Independent and Group

Objective: To develop students' understanding of history's influence on the present as well as the interconnectedness of world events, students must:

1. Summarize a recent world event.
2. Analyze the event's worldwide significance.
3. Apply knowledge of the country's history to the event.
4. Determine the event's potential consequences.
5. Evaluate the U.S. role (if any) in the event or in resolving it.

Materials: Internet access

Description: This assignment is designed to be recurrent throughout the course. It requires students to use news websites to research, interpret, and summarize events as classwork or a homework assignment. The oral presentations make this activity appropriate for auditory and kinesthetic learners.

Procedure: Students use the "world" or "international" section of websites such as www.nytimes.com, www.cnn.com, www.foxnews.com, or www.msnbc.msn.com to find an article about a significant world event (one having impact on one or more countries) that has recently occurred (you may wish to explicitly define "recently" for your students). Each student must then write an essay in which the student:

1. Summarizes the event.
2. Analyzes the event's worldwide significance.
3. Critiques the role that history plays in this event.
4. Evaluates the event's potential consequences.
5. Considers the U.S. role.
6. Provides an opinion on each of these factors.

The students divide into groups of three to five students.

1. Each student discusses his or her event as well as the website from which the article was chosen.
2. Then each group selects one event and a speaker who presents the paper to the class. The speaker need not be the writer of the essay.
3. The entire class then discusses the events, including students' reactions to the articles and to the opinions expressed in the essays. The students are required to defend their views with facts.

Differentiation: Gifted students might follow the assignment as designed. For regular education students, steps three and four of the essay may be omitted. For special education students, the essay may contain only steps one and six, depending upon the ability level of the students.

OVERVIEW: WORLD HISTORY ACTIVITY IV—TIME TRAVEL (ROLE-PLAYING)

Activity Type: Motivating or Building; Group

Objective: To introduce students to new concepts or to reinforce concepts through dramatizations, students must:

1. Strategize about how to present a historic event that is being studied.
2. Predict the outcomes of the actual event.
3. Dramatize the historic event.
4. Compare and contrast their dramatizations with the actual events.

Materials: None are needed, as students improvise with items that are readily available in the classroom.

Description: This is a role-playing activity, which may be repeated several times each week, as it lends itself to virtually any history lesson's development. The students use prior knowledge to predict the outcome of the historic event being studied, and then dramatize the event as they predicted. This highly participatory activity can serve as a catalyst for long-term learning. The teacher may use this role-playing activity in other history classes (U.S. history or European history) by adapting it to topics in that course.

Procedure: One role-playing example is for the students to recreate a battle in conjunction with a lesson on war. The battle is dramatized as follows:

1. The teacher designates two students as "generals."
2. Each general forms an army and strategizes for battle.
3. The battle occurs with students hurling paper balls as ammunition.
4. Students who are hit in the head or torso with the paper balls are considered to be "killed."
5. When everyone on one side has been killed, the battle ends.
6. The teacher explains the historic event and leads a discussion comparing and contrasting the dramatization with the historic battle.

Differentiation: Students automatically differentiate this activity without intervention by the teacher. The students do so via the amount of detail in their strategy and by analyzing the facts.

OVERVIEW: WORLD HISTORY PROJECT I—WHAT HAPPENED IN THE OLDEN DAYS? (ANCIENT CIVILIZATIONS)

Project Type: Building; Independent

Objectives: To apply students' cultural understanding of ancient civilizations, in a historical context, students must:

1. Research information.
2. Develop a research paper.
3. Formulate a timeline.
4. Create a visual or audio representation.

Description: Based on the ancient civilizations taught in class, this project provides a deeper study of their culture and history. The cultural research that the students gather becomes the basis for the paper and the timeline highlights the civilization's historic events. In addition, the students can express their originality through the visual or audio representations.

Procedure: Students must select an ancient civilization from the following five: Egypt, India, China, Greece, and Rome.

1. Each student researches the chosen civilization's culture and writes a paper about it.
2. Next, the student formulates a visually appealing timeline that indicates the civilization's historic events. The timeline's design should clearly reflect the civilization. Some examples are a scroll for Egypt, a sword for Rome, or oracle bones for China.
3. Each student must then create a visual representation of the civilization (a poster, costume, diorama, or other three-dimensional design) or an auditory representation (a song or a poem about the civilization). The students may become the visual by wearing costumes that they have created. They then must explain the costume's design significance. If the students choose to write a song or a poem, it must be performed in class.
4. The students must present the above three items in class.

Differentiation: The project would remain essentially the same for all ability levels, except that special education teachers may prefer to make this a small group project rather than an individual project.

HANDOUT: WORLD HISTORY PROJECT I—WHAT HAPPENED IN THE OLDEN DAYS?

Select one of the ancient civilizations that we have studied (Egypt, India, China, Greece, or Rome):

1. Create a timeline of the civilization's important historic events.
2. Type a _____-page report on the civilization's culture. The report must be _____-spaced, font size _____, font type _____, with a cover page, works cited page, and internal documentation. At least three works must be used, one of which must be a book.
3. Create a visual or audio representation of the civilization, such as a poster, three-dimensional display, song, poem, or costume. You may choose to be the visual representation and you must create the costume yourself. If you choose an audio representation such as a song or poem, it must be original and you must perform it yourself.
4. Present all three of the above in class.

RUBRIC: WORLD HISTORY PROJECT I—WHAT HAPPENED IN THE OLDEN DAYS?

Name _____

Grade _____

Scale: Excellent=5; Very Good=4; Good=3; Fair=2; Poor=1; Not Done=0

1. Research paper's format (25 points)_____
    A. Paper is at least _____ pages, _____-spaced (5 points)_____
    B. Font is size _____, type _____ (5 points)_____
    C. Includes cover page (5 points)_____
    D. Internal documentation is complete and accurate (5 points)_____
    E. Works cited page is complete and accurate (5 points)_____
2. Research paper's content (25 points)_____
    A. Covers one of the five civilizations (5 points)_____
    B. Describes the civilization (5 points)_____
    C. Covers only the B.C. period (5 points)_____
    D. Is comprehensive (5 points)_____
    E. Is well organized (5 points)_____
3. Timeline (15 points)_____
    A. Covers all major historic events (5 points)_____
    B. Is sequential (5 points)_____
    C. Shows effort/creativity (5 points)_____
4. Visual or audio (20 points)_____
    A. Is representative of the entire civilization (10 points)_____
    B. Shows effort and creativity (10 points)_____
5. Presentation (15 points)_____
    A. Speaks clearly (5 points)_____
    B. Shows knowledge of the content (5 points)_____
    C. Shows enthusiasm (5 points)_____

OVERVIEW: WORLD HISTORY PROJECT II—WHERE I WANT TO LIVE (CREATE A CIVILIZATION)

Project Type: Culminating; Group

Objectives: To apply and synthesize students' knowledge about ancient civilizations by inventing a fictitious civilization, students must:

1. Invent a civilization that includes the six common characteristics of a civilization.
2. Explain and describe the civilization in writing.
3. Design a three-dimensional representation.

Description: This kinesthetic activity requires students to utilize concepts and information gained in their study of ancient civilizations. They must apply this knowledge by developing their own civilization.

Procedure: Students work in groups of three to create and develop a fictitious civilization.

1. Each group must compose a paper that fully describes and explains their civilization. The paper must include the six basic characteristics of a civilization (government [including laws, penalties, economy], religion, writing or recordkeeping, art, social stratification, and cities near rivers).
2. Then the students must design a three-dimensional visual representation that contains buildings such as houses, schools, public works, and houses of worship; infrastructure and transportation; and landforms.
3. Each group presents the paper and the visual representation in class.
4. Each student later completes and submits a group self-assessment form in class.

Differentiation: Students of all ability levels can successfully complete this project as designed. The only measurable differentiation is that teachers of gifted classes might expect their students to write more detailed analyses of their civilizations.

HANDOUT: WORLD HISTORY PROJECT II—WHERE I WANT TO LIVE

Working in groups of three, you must create your own civilization. You must write a paper that explains and describes your civilization. There must also be a three-dimensional visual representation of the civilization. The project must contain:

1. All six characteristics of a civilization: government (with a military and an economic system); religion; cities near water; writing; art that includes architecture, technology and the fine arts; and social stratification. Both the paper and the visual representation must reflect all six of these characteristics.
2. The civilization's culture (including values, family structure, rules for marriage and family relationships, laws, holidays, celebrations, entertainment, food, and clothing) must be included in the paper and indicated—to the extent possible—in the visual representation.
3. The transportation, landforms and landscape, homes, businesses, places of worship, and public services (including police, fire, and sanitation) must also be included, along with representations of the people.

The paper and the visual must be presented in class by all group members.

RUBRIC: WORLD HISTORY PROJECT II—WHERE I WANT TO LIVE

Name _____

Grade _____

Grading Scale: Excellent=5; Very Good=4; Good=3; Fair=2; Little Effort=1; No Effort=0

  I. Group self-assessment (15 points) _____

 II. The paper's content (50 points)_____

    A. Fully describes the following (5 points each):

      1. Government (including army + economy + laws) _____

      2. Religion_____

      3. Cities_____

      4. Social stratification_____

      5. Writing_____

      6. Art (including fine arts, technology, architecture)_____

    B. Fully explains the culture including (5 points each):

      1. Values_____

      2. Family structure/family relationships_____

      3. Holidays/celebrations/entertainment_____

      4. Food/clothing_____

III. Visual representation (25 points)_____

    A. The following items are included (5 points each):

      1. Homes_____

      2. Landforms/landscape_____

      3. Transportation_____

      4. Businesses/public services _____

      5. Houses of worship_____

IV. Presentation (10 points)_____

    A. Completely explains the project_____

    B. Speaks clearly and enthusiastically _____

Group: Self-Assessment

Name: _____

Responsibility: _____

Grading Scale: 5=Excellent; 4=Very Good; 3=Good; 2= Fair; 1=Little Effort; 0=No Effort

Assessed By	Completed Assigned Work	Quality of Work	Participation Level	Worked with Others
1. SELF				
2.				
3.				
4.				
TOTALS				

Grade: _____

OVERVIEW: WORLD HISTORY PROJECT III—SO, WHAT ELSE HAVE YOU DONE? (BIOGRAPHY)

Project Type: Building; Independent

Objectives: To examine and analyze historic figures' lives, students must:

1. Research a historic person.
2. Describe the person's entire life.
3. Explain and evaluate the accomplishments that led to this person's fame.
4. Examine the long-term significance of this person's contributions.
5. Justify their choice of this person as interesting.

Description: For this project, students must describe and analyze any historic person who lived between the High Middle Ages and the present. Evaluation involves examining information, justifying decisions, drawing conclusions, and forming opinions.

Procedure: Each student must select a historic person that he or she considers "interesting."

1. The students research the historic person's life through the Internet and biographical books.
2. Then the students must write a biography that evaluates the person's contributions to history, including accomplishments as well as shortcomings. In the paper, the students must also strongly defend labeling this person as "interesting." They must also draw conclusions and make inferences supported by facts about the historic person.
3. Lastly, the students need to design a visual or audio representation that exemplifies the person's life.

Differentiation: The differentiation of this project is, once again, in the depth of information expected from the students, based upon their abilities. As a result, the teacher may decide to adjust the paper's length to fit the ability level of the students. For example, in gifted classes, the students' may be instructed to more critically analyze the impact of the person's contributions to history than might be expected by regular or special education classes, making the required length of the paper longer for the gifted classes.

Also, this project may be changed to fit other history courses by modifying the time period and requiring the students to choose subjects from the appropriate aspect of history (for example, only American subjects in a U.S. history course).

HANDOUT: WORLD HISTORY PROJECT III—SO, WHAT ELSE HAVE YOU DONE?

Select any interesting person (not an entertainer or athlete) who lived between the High Middle Ages and the present. You alone determine who is considered an interesting person. Then research this person's life, including accomplishments as well as shortcomings. Evaluate his or her contributions to history. Be sure to justify your reasons for considering this person to be interesting.

1. Develop a _____-page report about the person's entire life, from birth to death, encompassing all of the above information and any other information that you consider to be interesting or important about this individual.
2. The report must be _____-spaced, font size _____, font type _____. Internal documentation is required. You must also include a cover page and a works cited page, with a minimum of three works, one of which must be a book (not your textbook).
3. Create a visual or audio representation that exemplifies the person's life.
4. Present both the report and the visual or audio in class.

RUBRIC: WORLD HISTORY PROJECT III—SO, WHAT ELSE HAVE YOU DONE?

Name _____

Grade _____

1. The research paper's format (25 points) _____
   A. Font is size _____, type _____ (5 points) _____
   B. Internal documentation is correct and complete (5 points) _____
   C. Works cited page is correct and complete (5 points) _____
   D. Cover page is included (5 points) _____
   E. Paper is minimum of ____ pages, _____-spaced (5 points) _____
2. The research paper's content (40 points) _____
   A. The person's entire life is covered, including accomplishments and shortcomings (10 points) _____
   _____
   B. Evaluation of the person's contributions to history (10 points) _____
   C. Justification for choosing this person (10 points) _____
   D. Conclusions about and opinions of the person (10 points)_____
3. The visual or audio representation (20 points)_____
   A. Clearly represents the person's life (10 points) _____
   B. Quality of the visual or audio (10 points) _____
4. Presentation (15 points)_____
   A. Clearly explains the person's life (5 points)_____
   B. Shows knowledge of the subject (5 points)_____
   C. Shows enthusiasm (5 points)_____

OVERVIEW: WORLD HISTORY PROJECT IV—TELL ME A TRUE STORY (HISTORIC EVENT)

Project Type: Culminating; Group

Objectives: To analyze and synthesize information about a historic event, students must:

1. Research a historic event.
2. Analyze the event's causes and effects.
3. Recreate the event.
4. Appraise the event's significance in terms of modern history.

Description: This project entails researching and recreating a historic event. It provides kinesthetic learning as the students reenact the historic events or construct a three-dimensional representation of the event. As the students present their projects, they provide visual and auditory learning for their classmates.

Procedure: Working in groups of three, students research a historic event of their own choosing, that occurred between the Renaissance period and the present.

1. Students select a historic event from the assigned time period and research it.
2. Then each group writes a paper based on the research. The paper must describe and explain the event, analyze its causes and effects, and evaluate the event's impact on modern history.
3. Each group also has to create a visual representation of the event through drama, a movie or a three-dimensional design. Alternatively, students may choose to compose an audio representation of the event such as an original song or poem that the student must perform in class.
4. Each student later completes and submits a group self-assessment form in class.

Differentiation: Gifted students may successfully complete this project as designed, as can regular education classes, although you may wish to omit step five for the latter. For special education classes, you may prefer to enlarge the groups to four members to provide additional input for each group. Also, special education teachers may find it helpful to eliminate steps four and five.

Like the previous project, teachers can easily modify this one to suit other history courses by changing the time period and by requiring the events to be pertinent to that particular course of study.

HANDOUT: WORLD HISTORY PROJECT IV—TELL ME A TRUE STORY

Working in groups of three, you must re-create a significant event in history that occurred between the Renaissance period and the present. You must:

1. Type a _____-page paper explaining and describing the event. In the paper, you must analyze the event's causes and effects, as well as evaluate and interpret the event's impact on modern history. Be sure to include your own critique (with both positive and negative opinions).
2. Make sure that the paper is _____-spaced, font size _____, font type _____. The paper also must have internal documentation, a cover page and a works cited page with a minimum of three works, one of which must be a book. Your textbook does not count.
3. Create a visual or audio representation of the event such as a dramatization, a movie, a book, a diorama, a song, or a poem.
4. Complete the group self-assessment in class.
5. Present the paper and the visual or audio representation in class. All group members must participate.

RUBRIC: WORLD HISTORY PROJECT IV—TELL ME A TRUE STORY

Name _____

Grade _____

1. Group self-assessment grade (15 points) _____
2. The paper's format (25 points) _____
    A. Font is size _____, type _____ (5 points) _____
    B. Internal documentation is correct and complete (5 points) _____
    C. Works cited page is correct and complete (5 points) _____
    D. Cover page is included (5 points) _____
    E. Paper is minimum of _____ pages, _____-spaced (5 points) _____
3. The paper's content (35 points) _____
    A. Description and explanation of the event (8.75 points) _____
    B. Analysis of the causes and effects of the event (8.75 points) _____
    C. Interpretation of the event's impact on modern history (8.75 points) _____
    D. Critique of the event (8.75 points) _____
4. Visual or audio representation (15 points)_____
    A. Accurately represents the event (10 points) _____
    B. Quality and creativity of the visual or audio (5points) _____
5. Presentation (10 points) _____
    A. Shows knowledge of the event (5 points)_____
    B. Speaks clearly and with enthusiasm (5 points)_____

Group: Self-Assessment

Name: _____

Responsibility: _____

Grading Scale: 5=Excellent; 4=Very Good; 3=Good; 2= Fair; 1=Little Effort; 0=No Effort

Assessed By	Completed Assigned Work	Quality of Work	Participation Level	Worked with Others
1. SELF				
2.				
3.				
4.				
TOTALS				

Grade: _____

3

U.S. History

A year-long course for juniors, U.S. history typically covers every topic from Columbus's arrival to current issues in the United States. Since many of these topics have been taught in lower grades, students often think they already know all there is to know about the subject. The assignments in this chapter are meant to show the students otherwise.

First, the activities help to make U.S. history more participatory for the students. In three of the five activities, the students work in groups to reenact historic events. The caveat here is that the students recreate these events in whatever manner they believe the events occurred. However, this gives the teacher the opportunity to develop pertinent lessons that reveal where the errors lie in the students' versions of the events, thereby making the facts more memorable by comparison. An additional activity compels students to revisit history through the eyes of a virtual participant.

Unlike the activities, the five projects in this chapter require the students to work independently. Continuing the idea of having students express their own perspectives on important events in U.S. history, these projects compel the students to research topics that have been covered in class, but with a twist. Instead of merely repeating and expanding on what they've already learned in class, the students use these projects to highlight a different viewpoint on a well-known event.

With ten assignments, this chapter is the most extensive in the book, providing an opportunity for a more comprehensive study of U.S. history.

OVERVIEW: U.S. HISTORY ACTIVITY I—MAKING THE LAWS
(THE MAYFLOWER COMPACT, THE ARTICLES OF CONFEDERATION, AND THE CONSTITUTION)

Activity Type: Motivating; Group

Objective: To introduce students to the process of developing a government's laws, students must:

1. Propose ideas about how a school should effectively be run.
2. Construct classroom rules and consequences for violation of the rules.
3. Appraise the rules and consequences to determine which ones to enact.
4. Compare and contrast a school's government with a country's government.

Materials: Microsoft Word or PowerPoint

Description: In this activity, the school becomes a microcosm of the larger society. This activity may be done in conjunction with a lesson involving the formation of government. For example, the Mayflower Compact, the Articles of Confederation, and the Constitutional Convention are good topics. Students work cooperatively to develop rules for governing their classroom.

Procedure: Students work in small groups. Each group develops rules for governing the class by:

1. Discussing how schools maintain order.
2. Determining which rules are important for the effective functioning of a classroom.
3. Composing rules and consequences for the students of their classroom via Microsoft Word or PowerPoint.
4. Presenting their rules to the rest of the class.
5. Appraising the rules presented by each group to determine which rules to enact.
6. Voting to approve the rules.

The teacher then teaches a lesson about the formation of local and national governments, the potential pitfalls of a weak government (e.g., the Articles of Confederation) and the purpose of a constitution (highlighting the Bill of Rights).

Differentiation: For special education classes, the teacher may prefer to conduct the lesson prior to the activity. This would provide a clear context and something of a guideline for the students to develop in the activity. Teaching the lesson first would also make this a building activity, rather than a motivating activity.

OVERVIEW: U.S. HISTORY ACTIVITY II—SALE! SALE! SALE! (SLAVE AUCTIONS)

Activity Type: Building; Group

Objective: To broaden students' understanding of the slave trade, students must:

1. Construct sale posters.
2. Describe the skills of "slaves" offered for auction.
3. Judge each slave's value.
4. Experience being sold as property.
5. Analyze the process of slave auctions.
6. Draw conclusions about slavery's role in the U.S. economy of the time.

Materials: Paper, colored pencils or markers, a table

Description: This is a role-playing activity in which a slave auction is dramatized. It develops the concepts that the teacher has presented in a prior lesson on slavery.

Procedure: The students begin by preparing for the slave auction:

1. First, the students design posters to advertise the slave auction. The teacher displays the posters in the classroom.
2. The students then dramatize the auction. The dramatization is as follows:
   A. One student plays the role of auctioneer.
   B. Other students volunteer to be slaves.
   C. While standing on a table to make themselves visible to everyone, the "slaves" are sold, one at a time, as the auctioneer extols their abilities and worth.
   D. The remaining students then bid on each slave, with the slaves being sold to the highest bidders.
   E. The auction continues until all slaves have been sold.
3. After the auction, the teacher then conducts a class discussion on the slave trade, including slave markets and slavery's role in the U.S. economy.

Differentiation: Teachers might follow up this activity by using a novel in which slavery is a major theme (such as *Uncle Tom's Cabin*). Gifted classes might be directed to read the novel and then write a paper in which they assess the slave's position in U.S. society. Regular education and special education classes might be given excerpts of the book to which they would respond in class discussions.

OVERVIEW: U.S. HISTORY ACTIVITY III—THE DEBATE IS ON (LINCOLN V. DOUGLAS)

Activity Type: Building; Group

Objective: To evaluate the important issues that shaped the political debates between Abraham Lincoln and Stephen Douglas, students must:

1. Research the political issues surrounding the 1858 campaign for a U.S. senate seat from Illinois.
2. Scrutinize each candidate's view on the issues.
3. Formulate a debate strategy.
4. Debate the issues as a team.
5. Discuss the historic debate's impact on the politics of the time.

Materials: Access to the Internet and to a media center

Description: The students work in two groups (one for Lincoln and the other for Douglas) to research the candidates' views on the major issues related to slavery in 1858 and present them in a debate format. This activity could also be done in conjunction with lessons on the Compromise of 1850, popular sovereignty, slavery, or abolition, as these issues overlap those in this activity.

Procedure: This activity requires three class periods. Students might use one period for research, a second period for constructing the debate arguments, and the third period for the debate and discussion.

1. Prior to beginning the activity, the teacher should conduct a lesson that provides basic background information on the Lincoln-Douglas debates.
2. Then the teacher divides the class into two groups, one for each candidate. All students in each group work as a team both in preparing for the debate and in participating in the debate.
3. The students research the major issues surrounding slavery in 1858 and their candidate's views on the issues. The Internet and the media center are the sources for the research.
4. Then the students strategize about the arguments that they are presenting in the debate.
5. As the students develop their arguments they compose the arguments to be used in the debate.
6. The teacher then moderates a debate between the two teams.
7. After the debate, the teacher leads a class discussion about the results of the Lincoln-Douglas debate (which may differ from the results of the class debate) and the impact that the Lincoln-Douglas debate had on U.S. political history.

Differentiation: Teachers of gifted classes may expect the students to conduct a debate that encompasses all issues pertaining to slavery in 1858. Regular education teachers may select two or three issues for the students to research and debate. For special education classes, the teacher may prefer to have the students focus on one issue in detail.

OVERVIEW: U.S. HISTORY ACTIVITY IV—THE WAR AND ME (CIVIL WAR)

Activity Type: Building; Group

Objective: To analyze the impact of the U.S. Civil War on various groups in society, students must:

1. Research the societal role of a specific U.S. group before the Civil War.
2. Evaluate the two possible outcomes of the war and their potential impact on this group.
3. Present the circumstances and outcome of the war from a first-person perspective, as a member of this societal group.
4. Discuss the long-term consequences of the Civil War on this societal group.

Materials: Internet access

Description: As part of a unit on the Civil War, this activity builds on lessons that the teacher has already taught. As a result, students are compelled to view the war less as an abstract concept and more as a personal construct.

Procedure: This activity requires two class periods: one for research and one for presentation and discussion of the information.

1. Students work in pairs of their own choosing or as assigned by the teacher.
2. Each pair researches the societal role of one of the following groups before and during the Civil War: white northern men, white southern men, white northern women, white southern women, free African Americans, African American slaves, Native Americans. The teacher may randomly assign the groups or allow each pair to choose the group they research.
3. Together, each pair writes a first-person presentation representing a composite character based on their research. This presentation explains the experiences of the group through the eyes of this composite character and offers conjecture (based on facts) as to how the two possible outcomes of the war might affect members of this person's societal group.
4. The teacher facilitates a discussion on how the war's actual outcome has affected members of these societal groups.

Differentiation: Teachers of regular education classes may conduct the activity as designed. In gifted classes, teachers might instruct students to research an actual member of the group they researched. Students can then use this person's life to support or refute the contentions of the composite character. In special education classes, students may research a real person as assigned by the teacher rather than develop a composite character.

OVERVIEW: U.S. HISTORY ACTIVITY V—WELCOME TO AMERICA!
(IMMIGRATION TO THE UNITED STATES)

Activity Type: Building; Group

Objective: To introduce students to the immigrant experience on arrival in the United States during the period from 1892 to 1954, students must:

1. Analyze immigrants' arrival in the United States.
2. Evaluate the processing of immigrants.
3. Assess the problems encountered by immigrants.
4. Develop a dramatization.
5. Interpret immigrant experiences via role-play.

Materials: None

Description: The students dramatize the processing of immigrants at Ellis Island, based on a basic lesson on immigration that has already been taught.

Procedure: Several students play the role of inspectors and others play the immigrants.

1. The teacher instructs the inspectors to check each immigrant's paperwork and physical health. The inspectors must reject those whom they deem to be sick or lacking the proper credentials. For the purposes of this activity, students may arbitrarily reject anyone.
2. Inspectors take turns standing in the classroom's doorway while the immigrants stand in the hall.
3. As the inspector "processes" immigrants, each attempts to communicate with the other without speaking English. Students may speak other languages, create a language or use hand signals to communicate with each other.
4. Inspectors then determine whether each immigrant is allowed entrance into the United States (entrance into the classroom).
5. Upon entrance into the United States, immigrants are assigned to "live" in specific areas (of the classroom) as they are rejected when they seek admittance to other areas.
6. Immigrant names that are misunderstood by the inspectors are changed to names that sound more "American."
7. Immigrants who are refused entrance into the United States are asked to remain in the hall.
8. The rest of the students return to class and discuss the "processing."
9. The students in the hall then join the class and discuss their experiences.
10. The teacher then begins a unit on immigration, prejudice, discrimination, and stereotypes.

OVERVIEW: U.S. HISTORY PROJECT I—LIVING IN THE COLONIES (THE THIRTEEN ORIGINAL COLONIES)

Project Type: Building; Group or Independent

Objective: To apply and synthesize students' content knowledge about the thirteen original colonies, students must:

1. Research one colony, in depth.
2. Examine the colony's people and culture.
3. Assemble the information in a detailed paper.
4. Design and construct a visual representation of the colony.

Description: This project may be done independently or in a small group. Each student or group researches one colony. In so doing, the students must go beyond basic knowledge of each colony, by presenting information on the values, beliefs, and other influences on the people and culture of the colony that they are researching.

Procedure: The teacher ensures that all thirteen colonies are researched by assigning the colonies to the students or by requiring the students to sign up for the colonies.

1. Each student or group researches the following information: the reasons for the colony's formation, the manner in which the colony was governed, the colony's religion, and its social stratification.
2. Each student or group must then add additional information that reflects the uniqueness of the colony's people and culture.
3. The students then collate the information into a research paper.
4. The students must then design and construct a visual representation that mirrors the information in the paper and clearly distinguishes the colony from the others.
5. Each student or group then presents the paper and the visual representation.

Differentiation: In special education classes, teachers might modify steps one and two, by limiting the number of factors the students must research or by changing which factors they research.

HANDOUT: U.S. HISTORY PROJECT I—LIVING IN THE COLONIES

This project requires you to research life in one of the thirteen original colonies. Your research must focus on the colony's people and culture. The project has three parts:

1. A research paper that has _____ pages, (_____-spaced, font type_____, font size_____). The paper must include the following information: the reasons the colony was formed, the manner in which the colony was governed, the colony's religion, and its social stratification. You must also add information that reflects the qualities that make the colony unique. Make sure that your paper includes a cover page, a works cited page and internal documentation.

2. A visual representation that reflects the colony's distinctive characteristics as described in your paper. Your visual may be a three-dimensional design, a film, or a detailed painting. It must clearly distinguish this colony from all others. Effort and creativity count!

3. You must present the paper and the visual in class.

RUBRIC: U.S. HISTORY PROJECT I—LIVING IN THE COLONIES

Name _____

Grade _____

1. The paper's format (25 points) _____
   A. Font is size _____, type _____ (5 points) _____
   B. Internal documentation is correct and complete (5 points) _____
   C. Works cited page is correct and complete (5 points)_____
   D. Cover page is included (5 points) _____
   E. Paper is minimum of _____ pages, _____-spaced (5 points) _____
2. The paper's content (30 points)_____
   A. All required information is included (10 points) _____
   B. Comprehensive additional information about the colony's people and culture is included (10 points)___
      _____
   C. The colony's unique characteristics are fully described and explained (10 points) _____
      _____

3. Visual representation (35 points) _____
   A. Reflects the colony's distinctive characteristics as described in the paper (15 points) _____
      _____
   B. Is historically accurate (10 points) _____
   C. Shows effort and creativity (10 points)_____
4. Presentation (10 points)_____
   A. Shows knowledge of the colony (5 points) _____
   B. Speaks with expression and interest (5 points)_____

OVERVIEW: U.S. HISTORY PROJECT II—HOW THE WEST WAS SETTLED (WESTWARD EXPANSION)

Project Type: Culminating; Independent

Objective: To analyze westward expansion's effect on the region's people, students must:

1. Research the growth and development of a state that is west of the Mississippi River.
2. Compare and contrast the experiences of the Native Americans who lived on the land with the new settlers' experiences.
3. Collate the information into a research paper.
4. Create an original audio or visual presentation of either group's experiences.

Description: This project encourages students to study westward expansion from the perspectives of the people who experienced it: Native Americans and the new settlers. Therefore, this project is designed to be assigned at the end of a unit that includes such concepts as Manifest Destiny, the Oregon Trail, and the Trail of Tears. The students choose a state and specifically focus on the original inhabitants' experiences as well as the experiences of the people who settled there.

Procedure: The teacher allows the students to choose a state that is west of the Mississippi River.

1. Students research the Native Americans of their chosen state, as well as those who later settled on the land.
2. The students also research how the land became a state.
3. Next, the students formulate a research paper that is based on the research and compares and contrasts both groups' experiences. This should include how the two groups interacted with each other.
4. Students then devise a visual presentation or audio presentation (an original song, poem, or musical piece) that conveys the researched events from the perspective of either the Native Americans or the later settlers.
5. Students present the paper and the audio/visual in class.

Differentiation: Special education teachers may assign their students to work in pairs, with one student researching the Native American experiences and the other researching the new settlers' experiences. These pairs of students might then combine their efforts to develop the audio/visual presentation.

HANDOUT: U.S. HISTORY PROJECT II—HOW THE WEST WAS SETTLED

Before settlers moved west in the United States, Native Americans lived on the land. For this project, you must select a state that is west of the Mississippi River.

1. Research the Native Americans who originally lived there and the people who later settled there.
2. Your research should focus on the groups' cultures and lifestyles, their experiences living there, how they interacted with each other, how the land was settled, and how the land became a state.
3. Write a paper that describes your research and compares and contrasts the two groups. In addition to naming each Native American group, be sure to include the names of the most well-known settlers who later arrived.
4. The paper must be _____ pages long, _____-spaced, font type _____, and font size_____. Internal documentation, a works cited page and a cover page are also necessary.
5. Then, imagine yourself in the place of either the Native Americans or the later settlers. Create an audio (an original song, poem, or musical piece) or a visual (movie, skit, art) presentation that depicts either group's experiences, from their own perspective.
6. Present the paper and the audio or visual in class.

RUBRIC: U.S. HISTORY PROJECT II—HOW THE WEST WAS SETTLED

Name _____

Grade _____

1. The paper's format (25 points) _____
   A. Font is size _____, type _____ (5 points) _____
   B. Internal documentation is correct and complete (5 points) _____
   C. Works cited page is correct and complete (5 points) _____
   D. Cover page is included (5 points) _____
   E. Paper is minimum of _____ pages, _____-spaced (5 points) _____
2. The paper's content (40 points) _____
   A. Fully explains the settlement of the state (10 points)_____
   B. Completely describes the Native Americans and their culture (10 points)_____
   C. Accurately portrays the arrival of later settlers (10 points)_____
   D. Compares and contrasts the experiences of the Native Americans and the later settlers (10 points)_____
   _____
3. Audio or visual presentation (20 points) _____
   A. Presents the experiences solely from one group's perspective (10 points)_____
   B. Is historically accurate (10 points)_____
4. Presentation (15 points)_____
   A. Shows knowledge of the paper's content (5 points) _____
   B. Clearly links the paper and the audio/visual (5 points) _____
   C. Speaks with interest (5 points) _____

OVERVIEW: U.S. HISTORY PROJECT III—IF THE WAR HAD NEVER HAPPENED (MAJOR U.S. WARS)

Project Type: Culminating; Independent

Objective: To illustrate the impact war has had on U.S. history, students must:

1. Enumerate the causes of a major U.S. war.
2. Recount the main issues surrounding that war.
3. Examine that war's results.
4. Draw conclusions about how that war currently affects the United States.
5. Hypothesize about how the United States would have been changed if the war had not occurred.

Description: This project compels students to consider the effect of war. Unlike most other projects in this book, the students do not produce an audio or visual presentation. Instead, after the students present the projects, the class conducts an open forum on how different American life would be if the war had not occurred.

Procedure: The teacher instructs the students to select any major U.S. war that interests them.

1. Students research the war's causes, main issues, and results.
2. Then the students write a paper that encompasses all information that they researched.
3. The paper must also clearly delineate the student's idea on how the war impacted the United States and what the United States would be today had the war not occurred.
4. All students who research the same war present their papers on the same day, precluding the need for students to repeatedly present the same war's causes and issues.
5. The teacher allots time during each presentation period for an open forum on the students' views.

Differentiation: For special education classes, teachers may instruct half of the students to individually research one war and the other half of the class to research a different war. Limiting the assignment's breadth makes it easier for special education students with processing difficulties. The students might do the rest of the project as it is designed.

HANDOUT: U.S. HISTORY PROJECT III—IF THE WAR HAD NEVER HAPPENED

This project requires you to consider the effect that war has had on the United States. You must choose any war in which the United States has participated and write a paper about it.

1. The paper must explain the causes of the war, describe the issues surrounding the war, and analyze the war's results. You must also include your opinion on what the United States would be like today if that war had not occurred. Be sure to support your opinion with historically accurate information.
2. The paper must be _____ pages long, _____-spaced, with a font size_____, and font type _____. Include internal documentation, a cover page, and a works cited page.
3. You must present the paper in class, and then be able to defend your opinion as the class reacts to your paper during the class discussion time.

RUBRIC: U.S. HISTORY PROJECT III—IF THE WAR HAD NEVER HAPPENED

Name _____

Grade _____

1. The paper's format (25 points)_____
   A. Font is size _____, type _____ (5 points)_____
   B. Internal documentation is correct and complete (5 points)_____
   C. Works cited page is correct and complete (5 points) _____
   D. Cover page is included (5 points) _____
   E. Paper is minimum of _____ pages, _____-spaced (5 points) _____
2. The paper's content (60 points) _____
   A. The war's causes are fully explained (15 points)_____
   B. All issues surrounding the war are fully described (15 points)_____
   C. The war's results are fully and accurately analyzed (15 points) _____
   D. Facts are used to support opinion of how different the United States would be if the war had not occurred
      (15 points)_____
3. Presentation (15 points) _____
   A. Clearly explains the paper's content (5 points) _____
   B. Strongly defends your opinion (5 points)_____
   C. Speaks with interest (5 points) _____

OVERVIEW: U.S. HISTORY PROJECT IV—REVIEW OF A TWENTIETH-CENTURY DECADE (TWENTIETH-CENTURY AMERICA)

Project Type: Culminating; Independent

Objective: To analyze and interpret specific decades of twentieth-century U.S. history, students must:

1. Review one decade of U.S. history during the twentieth century.
2. Identify the U.S. government leaders of that decade.
3. Investigate U.S. economic and foreign policies during that decade.
4. Dissect the decade's significant U.S. events.
5. Examine U.S. popular culture during that decade.
6. Design a visual illustration that clearly depicts the decade.

Description: In this project, students use their knowledge of twentieth-century U.S. history coupled with research on that topic. The students use all information gathered to develop a paper and a visual depiction of a twentieth-century decade.

Procedure: Each student selects a decade of the twentieth century to research.

1. Students research the U.S. leaders, economic and foreign policies, four important events, and the popular culture of the decade.
2. Then each student writes a paper based on the information he or she gathered.
3. Each student then creates a visual interpretation of the decade. The students may choose to dress in period clothing to represent the decade.
4. The student presents the entire project in class.

Differentiation: Teachers of regular education classes may prefer to omit the research of economic and foreign policies. In addition to this omission, teachers of special education classes might also limit the research on important events to two instead of four.

HANDOUT: U.S. HISTORY PROJECT IV—REVIEW OF A TWENTIETH-CENTURY DECADE

Select any decade of the twentieth century and research the significant events pertaining to U.S. history and popular culture.

1. Write a paper about the major events of the decade as well as the significant cultural aspects of that decade in the United States The paper must be _____ pages long, _____-spaced, with font size____ and font type _____. You must have internal documentation, a cover page, and a works cited page.

2. Include the following:
    A. The U.S. president, vice president, secretary of state, defense secretary, treasury secretary, chief justice of the Supreme Court, our state senators, congressmen, and governor(s).
    B. A full explanation of the economic and foreign policies.
    C. The details of at least four significant events.
    D. A description of the decade's popular cultural events, including music, movies, books, television shows, clothing, and other entertainment.

3. Create a visual representation of the decade. You may be the visual.

4. Present the paper and visual in class. Effort and creativity count!

RUBRIC: U.S. HISTORY PROJECT IV—REVIEW OF A TWENTIETH-CENTURY DECADE

Name _____

Grade _____

1. Format of the paper (25 points) _____
   A. Font is size _____, type _____ (5 points) _____
   B. Internal documentation is correct and complete (5 points) _____
   C. Works cited page is correct and complete (5 points) _____
   D. Cover page is included (5 points) _____
   E. Paper is minimum of _____ pages, _____-spaced (5 points)_____
2. Content of the paper (40 points)_____
   A. All national and local leaders (as indicated on the handout) are included (10 points)_____

   _____
   B. Economic and foreign policies are described (10 points)_____
   C. Four significant U.S. events are analyzed (10 points)_____
   D. All aspects of U.S. popular culture are included (10 points)_____
3. Visual illustration (20 points)_____
   A. Clearly represents the decade (10 points) _____
   B. Shows effort and creativity (10 points)_____
4. Presentation (15 points)_____
   A. Shows knowledge of the content (5 points)_____
   B. Clearly explains the visual illustration (5 points)_____
   C. Speaks with interest (5 points)_____

OVERVIEW: U.S. HISTORY PROJECT V—A CHANGE IS COMING
(TWENTIETH-CENTURY PROTEST MOVEMENTS—CIVIL RIGHTS, WOMEN'S RIGHTS, VIETNAM)

Project Type: Culminating; Individual

Objective: To analyze the impetus for and impact of protest movements in U.S. society, students must:

1. Investigate the reasons for one protest movement.
2. Research pertinent U.S. laws.
3. Critique the leaders of this movement.
4. Analyze this movement's effect on one chosen leader.
5. Analyze this movement's effect on society.
6. Compare and contrast the views of the movement's participants with those of the opposition.
7. Collate the information into a research paper.

Description: This assignment is a study of the twentieth century's most significant protest movements and their enduring effects on U.S. culture and society. As a culminating assignment, it provides a more in-depth review of the use of the First Amendment right to freedom of speech via the civil rights movement, women's rights movement, and Vietnam protests.

Procedure: Students choose one of the following three protest movements to research: civil rights, women's rights, Vietnam.

1. Students use the Internet and at least one book source to research the issues surrounding this movement, the laws for and against the protesters, and the causes of the protests.
2. Students investigate the leaders of the protests and choose one to represent in his or her research paper.
3. Students study the opposition's leaders, their views, and tactics.
4. Students use Microsoft Word to write the paper from the perspective of the chosen protest leader.
5. Students explain the salient issues protested, the means of protest, and the reasons these methods were in keeping with First Amendment rights.
6. The paper must also directly refute opposing views (naming specific opponents).
7. Students present the papers in class.
8. The class votes on whether each presentation compels them to agree with the protestors or the opposition.

Differentiation: As described, this project is well-suited to gifted students. For regular education students, modification may not be needed, but teachers may prefer to have students explain the opposition's opinion rather than refute it. Teachers of special education students may want to limit the project to researching the movement and a few leaders.

HANDOUT: U.S. HISTORY PROJECT V—A CHANGE IS COMING

This project requires you to analyze the use of the First Amendment's freedom of speech in protest movements and the impact of a protest movement on the United States. You must research and write a paper about one of the following three protest movements: civil rights, women's rights, or Vietnam.

1. Use the Internet and at least one book source to research the issues surrounding this movement, the laws for and against the protesters, and the causes of the protests.
2. Investigate the leaders of the protests and choose one to represent in your research paper.
3. Study the opposition's leaders, their views, and tactics.
4. Write in first-person, from the perspective of your chosen protest leader. Be as persuasive as possible.
5. Explain the significant issues of the protest, the means of protest, and the reasons these methods were in keeping with First Amendment rights.
6. Directly refute opposing views (naming specific opponents).
7. Make sure that your paper is a minimum of _____ pages, _____-spaced. Use font type_____, size_____. Include a cover page, internal documentation of your sources, and a works cited page.
8. Present the paper in class.
9. After each presentation, the class votes to support either the protestor or the protestor's opponents.

RUBRIC: U.S. HISTORY PROJECT V—A CHANGE IS COMING

Name _____

Grade _____

1. Format of the paper (25 points) _____
    A. Font is size _____, type _____ (5 points) _____
    B. Internal documentation is correct and complete (5 points) _____
    C. Works cited page is correct and complete (5 points) _____
    D. Cover page is included (5 points) _____
    E. Paper is minimum of _____ pages, _____-spaced (5 points)_____
2. The paper's content (60 points)_____
    A. The issues and causes of the protest movement are fully described (10 points)_____
    B. The laws pertaining to this issue are fully discussed (10 points)_____
    C. The paper is written in first-person, from the perspective of a protestor in this same movement (10 points)
    _____
    D. The opposition's views are directly and fully refuted (10 points)_____
    E. The reasons this means of protest is in keeping with first amendment rights are clearly explained (10 points)
    _____
    F. The paper is persuasive (10 points)_____
3. Presentation (15 points) _____
    A. Clearly explains the paper's content (5 points) _____
    B. Strongly defends your opinion (5 points) _____
    C. Speaks with interest (5 points) _____

4

U.S. Government

U.S. government is a one-semester course usually taught to seniors. Since the main topics covered in this course are the Constitution and the government's formation, policies, and responsibilities (of all three branches), the assignments in this chapter are designed to build on these basic concepts.

These seven assignments are intended to produce deeper analysis of the topics and concepts, centered on the influences *of* and *on* the three branches of government. The idea is to compel the students to view government through a practitioner's eyes.

Unlike previous chapters, all of the projects are independent tasks, as is one of the activities. As a result, this chapter has fewer assignments than the preceding chapters. Being independent undertakings, these assignments require the students to do more individualized research, which also results in the students spending more time on the assignments.

Focusing on this type of individualized effort helps to prepare twelfth-grade students for college courses, which have a similar focus. In keeping with this collegiate bent, two of the three projects in this chapter involve no visual illustrations, as these are not commonly required in college courses.

OVERVIEW: GOVERNMENT ACTIVITY I—WHO'S IN CHARGE? (THE PURPOSE OF GOVERNMENT)

Activity Type: Motivating; Group

Objectives: To demonstrate the purpose and means of governing, students must:

1. Develop rules for governing their school.
2. Form a consensus on acceptable means of ruling and enforcing the rules.
3. Vote on the rules they enact.
4. Determine the consequences for violation of rules.
5. Collate the final rules into a published constitution.
6. Draw conclusions regarding central rule versus group rule (i.e., Federalists versus Anti-Federalists).

Materials: Microsoft Word or PowerPoint

Description: This activity, designed to begin a lesson on the role of government, requires students to devise rules for governing all students in the school. The goal is to give the students a basic understanding of the need for government as well as the means of governing. As such, this activity lends itself to a discussion of Federalists versus Anti-Federalists, the weaknesses of the Articles of Confederation, and the need for the United States to develop the Constitution.

Procedure: This lesson may last one to two periods, depending upon the amount of time the teacher chooses to allot for discussion. The teacher begins by informing the class that they must now develop rules for governing the students in their school.

1. The teacher divides the class into two groups: one group who favors a set of rules enforced by school administrators (i.e., Federalists) and a second group who favors rules established by each teacher (i.e., Anti-Federalists). If enough students don't genuinely hold these opinions, the teacher may assign students.
2. Each group devises rules of behavior and consequences for violation of the rules, which they compose into a list using Microsoft Word. Alternatively, the students may format the list as a PowerPoint presentation.
3. Each group reads its list of rules and consequences to the class as the teacher lists them on the board.
4. All students then vote on which rules and consequences are accepted.
5. The approved rules become the constitution.
6. The teacher then relates the activity to the formation of national governments.
7. Ideally, the constitution is comprised of rules from both groups, thereby leading the teacher into the lesson. The lesson should include the definition, purpose, types (autocracy, oligarchy, and democracy), and means (constitutional, totalitarian, and authoritarian) of governing. Subsequent lessons should include: the concepts of Federalists and Anti-Federalists, the perils of a weak government (e.g., Articles of Confederation), the need for the Constitution, and the reason for the addition of the Bill of Rights.

Differentiation: For regular education classes, the lesson is conducted as indicated. Teachers of special education students might conduct this lesson over three class periods. The first period is for the activity, the second period is the lesson tying the activity to the specific government concepts, and the third lesson reinforces the specific terms and concepts, allowing students sufficient time to complete each aspect of the activity.

In addition to this lesson, teachers of gifted students might do a variation of this assignment as a building activity. Having already learned the concepts indicated in step seven of this lesson, students apply them in a new context. In the building activity, the teacher divides the class into three groups, based on the three government types (students draw cards with a government type on it). Once formed, a representative from each of two groups may then choose an additional card to indicate the means of governing the group must employ (the democracy is automatically constitutional). Students then create rules for a fictional country based on their group's type and means of governing. They present these, and compare and contrast them with the United States.

OVERVIEW: GOVERNMENT ACTIVITY II—HAVING YOUR DAY IN COURT (FIFTH AND SIXTH AMENDMENTS)

Activity Type: Building; Group

Objectives: To demonstrate how the U.S. Constitution's Fifth and Sixth Amendments are implemented, students must:

1. Create an original criminal court case.
2. Role-play the case that they have designed.
3. Judge the case and reach a verdict.
4. Evaluate the role of the Fifth and Sixth Amendments in the case.

Materials: None

Description: This activity calls for students to develop and dramatize an original criminal court case. This gives the students a better understanding of the way the Constitution's Fifth and Sixth Amendments work.

Procedure: The entire class participates in this activity during two or three class periods.

1. First, the teacher teaches a lesson on the Constitution.
2. Then the teacher divides the class in half. One half of the class (Group One) creates a criminal court case and the other half (Group Two) becomes the jurors, lawyers, and judge in the case.
3. The teacher explains the responsibilities of the judge, lawyers, and jurors to Group Two while Group One is developing the court case.
4. Group Two then votes to select the two lawyers (one defense attorney and one prosecutor) and the judge.
5. After Group One apprises the lawyers of the court case's basic premise, the lawyers interview the remaining members of Group Two to determine who the jurors are.
6. Both groups then conduct the court case and reach a verdict.
7. Then the teacher leads a class discussion on how the Fifth and Sixth amendments apply to this case.

Differentiation: Special education teachers might work with the entire class to develop the court case rather than divide the class in half. In this case, all students present would vote for the students who would play the roles of judge, jurors, and lawyers. The rest of the activity would proceed as described above. Regular education and gifted classes would proceed as described.

OVERVIEW: GOVERNMENT ACTIVITY III—DEAR CONGRESS . . . (CONGRESSIONAL BILLS)

Activity Type: Motivating, Independent

Objectives: To review and evaluate the bills that Congress passes each week, students must:

1. Examine congressional bills.
2. Analyze one bill.
3. Summarize the bill.
4. Evaluate the impact of the bill.
5. Critique the bill.

Materials: Internet access

Description: This is designed to be a weekly activity which the teacher may assign for homework or as classwork. Each week the students check congressional websites and select one bill to report on, in an essay. Ultimately, the students express their views directly to Congress.

Procedure: Students check www.senate.gov or www.house.gov weekly.

1. Each student selects one bill that he or she finds interesting.
2. The student writes an essay that summarizes the bill, indicates when and by whom the bill was introduced, and tells how the student's senator or congressional representative voted on the bill. The essay must also include the student's assessment of the bill's impact, as well as the student's opinion of the bill.
3. The students read the bills aloud in class and offer reactions to them.
4. After the students have done this activity for about three months, the teacher sets aside a class period in which the students e-mail their senator or congressional representative. The students use this e-mail to respectfully express their opinions about the bills that have been studied and about the manner in which this senator or representative has voted.
5. If the students receive responses to the e-mails, they read them in class.

Differentiation: There are several modifications that special education teachers might use in their classes. First, these teachers might find it more beneficial to the students to do this activity solely as classwork, and to do it on a monthly basis rather than weekly. As classwork, the teacher would need access to enough computers for the entire class. This would enable the teacher to facilitate the activity by having all students use the same website and examine the bills as a class.

OVERVIEW: GOVERNMENT ACTIVITY IV—LET'S MAKE A DEAL (FORMING TREATIES AND OTHER FOREIGN POLICIES)

Activity Type: Culminating; Group

Objectives: To apply and synthesize students' foreign policy knowledge, students must:

1. Examine U.S. foreign policy and its changes over time.
2. Investigate the current foreign policy of a country other than the United States.
3. Study major issues currently affecting that country's relationship with other countries.
4. Develop a plan for addressing those issues.
5. Negotiate treaties.

Materials: Internet access

Description: This activity needs two class periods. It compels students to consider the methodology and skills needed to develop a foreign policy, including the creation of treaties.

Procedure: The teacher divides the class into four groups.

1. Then the teacher writes the names of the United States and three other countries on separate index cards.
2. A representative from each group randomly selects one index card. The group is known thereafter as the country that is indicated on the chosen card.
3. Each country uses the Internet to research the country's foreign policy from its inception to the present, as well as the major issues currently facing the country in relation to other countries.
4. Each country then develops a plan (foreign policy) for solving the issues.
5. The four countries meet to discuss their plans and to negotiate agreements (treaties) that enable the countries to peacefully coexist.
6. The teacher leads a discussion of the students' methodologies for developing their foreign policies and negotiating the treaties.

Differentiation: Special education teachers might divide their classes in half rather than into four groups. One group would represent the United States and the other group would represent any another country with whom the United States has ties. The rest of the activity can be carried out as outlined above.

OVERVIEW: GOVERNMENT PROJECT I—WHO HAS THE POWER? (POLITICAL ACTION COMMITTEES)

Project Type: Building; Independent

Objectives: To evaluate and synthesize information about political action committees (PACs), students must:

1. Explore the primary issues and ideologies of two PACs.
2. Investigate the methods of these PACs.
3. Describe each PAC.
4. Compare and contrast the two PACs.
5. Critique and analyze each group.

Description: In this project, students learn how political action committees influence public policy. The students need to investigate two different PACs and explain their beliefs and tactics, along with a critical analysis of the two organizations.

Procedure: Students select two PACs from a list provided by the teacher or two others that the teacher has approved.

1. Students research each organization to determine their constituency, ideologies, and methods for gaining passage of their public policy.
2. Students write a paper that contains all information obtained in step one, describes both PACs, compares and contrasts them, and critically analyzes them.
3. The students must also design a public notice for one of the PACs, using the same tactics employed by that organization, such as a television commercial, radio ad, billboard, or a fundraising letter.

Differentiation: For regular education classes, teachers may limit the assignment to the investigation of only one PAC. This would then eliminate the comparison portion of the paper. Special education teachers could make the same modifications as the regular education teachers. They might also focus the essay solely on explaining the constituency and ideology of the PAC.

HANDOUT: GOVERNMENT PROJECT I—WHO HAS THE POWER?

Select two political action committees (special interest groups) from the attached list. Research the groups and the tactics they employ to obtain passage of their public policy.

1. Include a description of each group, its constituency, and its ideology.
2. Compare and contrast the methods used by each group regarding public policy.
3. Provide your own analysis and opinion of each group.
4. The paper must be a minimum of _____pages, _____-spaced, font size ___, font type _____. Be sure to include internal documentation, a cover page, and a works cited page.
5. Create a visual representation of one group's methodology. For example, you might develop a television commercial, radio ad, billboard, or letter.
6. Present the paper and visual in class.

Special Interest Groups

AARP	MADD
ACLU	MoveOn.org
AFL–CIO	NAACP
AFT	National Abortion Rights Action League
American Arab Anti-Discrimination Committee	National Association of Counties
American Bar Association	National Association of Manufacturers
American Coalition of Citizens with Disabilities	National Audubon Society
American Jewish Congress	National Coalition to Ban Handguns
American Legion	National Congress of American Indians
American Psychological Association	National Council of Churches
American Tobacco Institute	National Council on the Aging
American Veterans Committee	National Farmers' Organization
Anti-Defamation League of B'nai B'rith	National Governors' Association
Center for Auto Safety	National League of Cities
Chamber of Commerce of the United States	National Right to Life Committee
Children's Defense Fund	National Urban League
Common Cause	NOW
Congress Watch	NRA
Council of Large Public Housing Authorities	Sierra Club
Cousteau Society	Union of Concerned Scientists
Georgia Peanut Association	Veterans of Foreign Wars
League of Conservative Voters	Water Pollution Control Federation
League of Women Voters	

RUBRIC: GOVERNMENT PROJECT I—WHO HAS THE POWER?

Name _____

Grade _____

1. Research paper (60 points)_____
    A. Paper is at least _____ pages, _____-spaced, font size___, font type_____(10 points)_____
    _____
    B. Paper has correct internal documentation (10 points)_____
    C. Cover page and works cited page are correct (10 points)_____
    D. Each group is fully described (10 points)_____
    E. The groups are fully compared and contrasted (10 points) _____
    F. Paper includes opinion and full analysis of each group (10 points) _____
2. Visual (25 points) _____
    A. Represents the group using their methodology (15 points)_____
    B. Is visually appealing (5 points)_____
    C. Is creative (5 points)_____
3. Oral presentation (15 points) _____
    A. Shows knowledge of the groups (5 points)_____
    B. Speaks clearly (5 points) _____
    C. Speaks with interest (5 points) _____

OVERVIEW: GOVERNMENT PROJECT II—WHOSE SIDE ARE YOU ON? (U.S. SUPREME COURT CASES)

Project Type: Culminating; Independent

Objectives: To examine and interpret the Supreme Court's responsibilities, students must:

1. Examine a current Supreme Court case.
2. Scrutinize all pertinent information about the case.
3. Prepare an argument.
4. Produce a decision on the case.

Description: This project enables students to clearly understand both sides of a Supreme Court case. It places students in the positions of both lawyer and Supreme Court Justice as the students first argue for one side of a case, and then render a decision in contradiction of that argument.

Procedure: Using the website www.onthedocket.org/cases or a similar website, each student selects a case that is on the U.S. Supreme Court docket but has not yet been argued.

1. The students must review all lower court briefs and decisions on the case.
2. After choosing which side of the case to represent, each student takes on the role of attorney and writes a brief or amicus curiae in support of that side.
3. Then the student, acting as a Supreme Court Justice, must write a decision in opposition to the brief or amicus.
4. Students must include references to all pertinent cases and constitutional amendments when writing both the brief and the decision.
5. Students present their work in class.

Differentiation: Special education teachers might omit step three. Also, these teachers might modify step four and require the students to indicate only the related constitutional amendments.

HANDOUT: GOVERNMENT PROJECT II—WHOSE SIDE ARE YOU ON?

Using the website www.onthedocket.org/cases (or another applicable website), research a case of interest to you that is currently on the Supreme Court docket.

1. Write a full description of the case.
2. Determine which side you are on and, as an attorney before the Supreme Court, write a brief or amicus curiae for that side.
3. Then, as a Supreme Court justice, write a decision in opposition to your brief or amicus curiae.
4. Make sure that both the brief and the decision express strong opinions and include references to all pertinent articles and/or amendments of the Constitution as well as any previous related court cases.
5. Include a copy of the actual case.

The entire project must be presented in class.

RUBRIC: GOVERNMENT PROJECT II—WHOSE SIDE ARE YOU ON?

Name _____

Grade _____

1. The case (30 points)_____
   A. A current Supreme Court case is presented (10 points)_____
   B. A copy of the case is included (10 points)_____
   C. The case is fully described (10 points)_____
2. The brief or amicus curiae (30 points)_____
   A. Strongly supports one side (10 points)_____
   B. Cites other pertinent cases (10 points)_____
   C. Is logical and sequential (10 points)_____
3. The decision (20 points)_____
   A. Firmly opposes the brief or amicus curiae (10 points)_____
   B. Constitutional support included for this decision is clearly pertinent to this case (10 points)_____
   _____

4. Presentation (20 points)_____
   A. Explains the case comprehensively (10 points)_____
   B. Speaks with interest (10 points)_____

OVERVIEW: GOVERNMENT PROJECT III—WHO ARE YOU VOTING FOR? (PRESIDENTIAL ELECTIONS)

Project Type: Building; Independent

Objectives: To apply critical thinking to the evaluation of presidential candidates, students must:

1. Investigate the candidate for whom they would vote for president of the United States.
2. Scrutinize the candidate's stand on the major issues.
3. Examine the opponent and his or her stand on the major issues.
4. Write a critical analysis of both candidates.

Description: In this project, students must, as fully and objectively as possible, dissect the views and planned policies of the Democratic and Republican nominees for president. They must then write a paper that not only delineates the candidates' views, but also explains which of the opponent's views the student agrees with as well as the demographic factors that play a role in the student's decision.

Procedure: The students research the views of the Republican and Democratic nominees for president.

1. Each student examines the stances and planned policies of the presidential candidate for whom they would vote for president.
2. Then the students research the same information about that candidate's opponent.
3. Each student must then write a paper. The first part of the paper must indicate whom they would choose for president, the reasons for that decision (including demographics), and the candidate's position on the important issues.
4. The second portion of the paper must explain the opponent's views and planned policies. Then the students must explain why they would not vote for this candidate, but must also describe areas of agreement with the candidate.
5. The students present their papers in class.
6. The teacher leads a discussion of the candidates and holds a mock election.

Differentiation: Special education classes might research only the candidate for whom they would not vote and explain the areas of agreement. Doing this would still enable the students to acquire a new perspective on the candidate.

HANDOUT: GOVERNMENT PROJECT III—WHO ARE YOU VOTING FOR?

You might know who you want to vote for, but this project is designed to make you question your decision. You must use the Internet to research the views and the policies that your chosen candidate intends to implement. Then you must do the same for your candidate's opponent. You must then write a paper that contains the following:

1. Full and unbiased account of your candidate's views and plans.
2. Explanation of your reasons for choosing this candidate.
3. Complete and objective description of the opposing candidate's views and plans.
4. Areas of agreement with the opponent.

The paper must be _____ pages long, _____-spaced, with size ___ font, and font type _____.
Internal documentation, a cover page, and a works cited page must be included.

   The paper must be presented in class.

RUBRIC: GOVERNMENT PROJECT III—WHO ARE YOU VOTING FOR?

Name _____

Grade _____

1. The paper's format (25 points) _____
   A. Font is size _____, type _____ (5 points) _____
   B. Internal documentation is correct and complete (5 points) _____
   C. Works cited page is correct and complete (5 points)_____
   D. Cover page is included (5 points)_____
   E. Paper is minimum of _____ pages, _____-spaced (5 points)_____
2. The paper's content (60 points)_____
   A. Full and accurate description of your candidate's views and policies (15 points)_____
   _____
   B. Detailed explanation of your reasons for choosing this candidate (15 points)_____
   _____
   C. Full and accurate description of the opposing candidate's views and policies (15 points)_____
   _____
   D. Detailed description of the areas in which you agree with the opponent (15 points)_____
   _____
3. Presentation (15 points)_____
   A. Clearly explains the paper's content (5 points)_____
   B. Expresses your own opinions (5 points)_____
   C. Speaks with interest (5 points)_____

5

Economics

In an economics course, high school seniors learn basic economic principles and the application of these principles to their own lives. Therefore, each assignment in this chapter is intended to do the same. From supply and demand to entrepreneurship to living within a budget, the activities and projects offered here put the students in everyday situations involving economic factors.

This chapter's goal is to take a subject that many students find tedious and boring, and make it interesting and relevant as they discover how economics fits into their daily lives. Each of the activities in this chapter has an aspect that sets it apart from activities in previous chapters. The first activity involves creating an actual school store that the students continue to run long beyond that semester. The second activity is unique in that it incorporates Microsoft's Excel spreadsheet, thereby adding a mathematical component to the project. In less dramatic fashion, the third activity has a graphic organizer whose information must be researched and filled in by the students as they gather the information.

The projects in this chapter are a bit different, too. The first difference is that projects I and II build on each other. In project I, the students design a business, which they then market in project II. The second difference is that the projects are designed to be accessible to all ability levels. Therefore, this chapter's projects contain little differentiation.

OVERVIEW: ECONOMICS ACTIVITY I—THE CLASS STORE (SUPPLY AND DEMAND)

Activity Type: Building; Group

Objectives: To apply the laws of supply and demand to running a business, students must:

1. Plan a store's creation and management.
2. Determine how to raise capital to fund this activity.
3. Choose the items to be sold.
4. Develop advertising for the store.
5. Use the laws of supply and demand to set prices and determine what items continue to be available for sale.

Materials: Items to be sold in the store

Description: This activity may require permission from the school district since it involves setting up and running an actual store, as well as holding fundraisers to gain the capital to start the store. As such, it is an ongoing activity that could continue for years. Students must learn how the laws of supply and demand establish what items they offer for sale and the price for each item.

Procedure: The teacher first teaches a lesson on supply and demand.

1. Then the teacher directs the class to use their basic knowledge of supply and demand to develop and manage a store.
2. First, the teacher leads the class in brainstorming about items to sell, fundraisers that can raise the capital to fund the store's opening, the business hours for the store, a schedule for everyone working in the store, and advertising for the store.
3. Then the students hold the fundraisers with the teacher's help.
4. The students, along with the teacher, use the capital gained from the fundraisers to purchase goods for the store.
5. Students, with the teacher's guidance, set prices for all items. In determining the prices, the students consider how to obtain the highest profit and still maintain the demand for the product.
6. The students then advertise the store to the rest of the student body.
7. Lastly, the students and teacher work in the store. They determine which items continue to be available for purchase (the supply) based on customer demand.

Differentiation: The only differentiation required here is that the teacher may need to provide greater oversight for special education classes for such tasks as handling money.

OVERVIEW: ECONOMICS ACTIVITY II—HOW TO BECOME A MILLIONAIRE (STOCK MARKET)

Activity Type: Building; Independent and Group

Objectives: To develop students' understanding of the stock market via participation in virtual purchases of stock, students must:

1. Study specific companies that are members of the New York Stock Exchange.
2. Develop a personal stock portfolio.
3. Monitor stock developments.
4. Buy and sell stocks based on current information.
5. Compare and compete with classmates for the most successful portfolio.

Materials: Internet access, Microsoft Excel or a notebook and pen

Description: This activity supports student comprehension of the stock market and promotes their participation in it.

Procedure: The students use free websites such as www.wallstreetsurvivor.com or vse.marketwatch.com/Game/Homepage.aspx.

1. The teacher allots each student a specific amount of money to be spent on the purchase of stocks.
2. Students research companies to discover the type of business, the company's financial success, the company's philosophy or mission (e.g., environmentally or socially active), and any other information that the students consider to be personally significant. They must keep a record of the information that they obtain.
3. Then each student maintains a list of the companies that he or she chooses to invest in.
4. The students buy shares of stock in their chosen companies.
5. On their own time, the students monitor the stocks daily to check progress or lack thereof. They'll maintain a record of their findings.
6. In keeping with the adage, "buy low, sell high," students sell stocks as they deem necessary and make additional purchases accordingly.
7. Once a week, the students update their classmates on the state of their individual portfolios.
8. At the end of the semester, the student with the most successful (highest earning) portfolio will be considered the winner. The teacher may award a predetermined prize.

Differentiation: Special education teachers may want to limit the number of companies in the students' portfolios and may also find it advantageous to limit the companies to one business field such as technology or health. In addition, these teachers may prefer to eliminate step five, and put steps six and seven together so that the entire activity is done in class.

OVERVIEW: ECONOMICS ACTIVITY III—LET'S GO SHOPPING (CONSUMERISM)

Activity Type: Building; Independent

Objectives: To demonstrate knowledge of effective consumer spending, students must:

1. List items to be purchased.
2. Compare prices of items.
3. Appraise the items' value.
4. Work within a fixed budget.
5. "Purchase" required items.

Materials: Internet access or catalogs, the handout, pens or pencils

Description: This activity encourages the students to become efficient consumers. Working within a budget, the students buy appropriate gifts for a list of people, while still having enough money to purchase a desired item for themselves.

Procedure: This activity can be done in conjunction with a lesson on consumerism or with a holiday such as Christmas.

1. The teacher allots each student a specific amount of money.
2. Then the teacher distributes the handout and instructs the students to stay within the budget.
3. Students purchase gifts for four different people, in honor of particular occasions. They must have enough money remaining to purchase a desired item for themselves. Appropriate examples of occasions for gifts are: a friend's birthday, a new baby in the family, a boyfriend or girlfriend's Valentine's gift, Mother's or Father's Day, and Christmas.
4. The students list the items that they plan to purchase. They may use the back of the handout for this list.
5. Students then use a search engine such as www.google.com to access websites of appropriate stores where they shop for the gifts.
6. The students use their lists to comparison shop for the items at different websites. They then compare the prices and the quality of the merchandise offered.
7. Students add this information to the list along with the prices of the items.
8. Students then "purchase" the items that they deem to be the best value for the price. This involves each student completing the handout.
9. Then each student subtotals the purchases, calculates the necessary tax, and totals the sale.
10. Students then report their purchases to the class.
11. Afterwards, the teacher leads a discussion on what makes an effective consumer.

Differentiation: This very basic activity is accessible to all ability levels and does not require differentiation.

Graphic Organizer: Economics Activity III—Let's Go Shopping

Name_____

Item	Store	Cost

Subtotal _____

Tax (___ %) _____

Total _____

OVERVIEW: ECONOMICS ACTIVITY IV—MONEY MAKES THE WORLD GO 'ROUND (CURRENT EVENTS)

Activity Type: Building; Independent and Group

Objectives: To develop students' understanding of the interconnectedness of world events and money, students must:

1. Summarize a recent world event.
2. Analyze the event's worldwide significance.
3. Apply knowledge of economics (using correct terminology) and the role of economic factors in this event.
4. Determine the event's potential consequences.
5. Evaluate the U.S. role (if any) in the event or in resolving it.

Materials: Internet access, Microsoft Word

Description: This assignment is designed to be recurrent throughout the course. It requires students to use news websites to research, interpret, and summarize events as classwork or a homework assignment. The oral presentations make this activity appropriate for auditory and kinesthetic learners.

Procedure: Each student uses the "national" and "international" section of Internet websites such as www.nytimes.com, www.cnn.com, www.foxnews.com, or www.msnbc.msn.com to find an article about a recent event with economic implications. Each student must then write an essay in which the student:

1. Summarizes the event.
2. Analyzes the event's national or international significance.
3. Critiques the role that economics plays in this event.
4. Evaluates the event's potential consequences.
5. Considers the U.S. role.
6. Provides an opinion on each of these factors.

The students divide into groups of three to five students.

1. Each student discusses his or her event, the economic factors, and his or her opinion.
2. Then each group selects one event and a speaker who presents the paper to the class. The speaker need not be the writer of the essay.
3. The entire class then discusses the events presented, the economic issues, students' reactions to the articles, and the opinions expressed in the essays. The students are required to defend their views with facts.

Differentiation: Gifted students might follow the assignment as designed. For regular education students, the essay may mention specific economic concepts in the event rather than critique the role of economics. For special education students, the essay might be limited to steps one and six as well as the same modification of the essay as indicated for the regular education students.

OVERVIEW: ECONOMICS PROJECT I—OPEN FOR BUSINESS (ENTREPRENEURSHIP/SOLE PROPRIETORS)

Project Type: Building; Independent

Objectives: To create and develop a business plan, students must:

1. Formulate an idea for a business.
2. Design a plan for the business.
3. Describe the business's clientele.
4. Determine a method for advertising the business.
5. Persuade an audience to support the business.
6. Explain government policies that may impact this business (e.g., laws pertaining to anti-trust, fair trade, monopolies).

Description: In this project, each student develops a plan to become an entrepreneur. The students design a "dream" business and persuade an audience that the business can genuinely be feasible.

Procedure: The teacher instructs the students to create a business that they believe would be lucrative as well as enjoyable to run.

1. Each student designs a plan for developing a business. The plan must include a name for the business, a means for raising capital for the business, details on the potential clientele, and the reasons that the business appeals to its clientele.
2. The students must also explain the viability of their businesses and their plans to make their businesses financially successful.
3. The students must also include a plan for marketing their businesses to the public.
4. Each student makes a persuasive presentation of his or her project in class. The presentation's purpose is to convince the audience of the business's viability.
5. The class members pose questions that the presenter should be prepared to answer.
6. Then the class reacts to each presentation in terms of whether the business could genuinely succeed in "real life." Their decision determines whether the business receives a "thumbs up" or "thumbs down."
7. The students vote for the most viable business and the winner receives a predetermined prize.

Differentiation: For students in special education classes, teachers might modify the assignment to include fewer details in steps one and two.

HANDOUT: ECONOMICS PROJECT I—OPEN FOR BUSINESS

In this project, you plan to become an entrepreneur as you design your "dream" business. This business may be a type that already exists or one that you wish existed. The plan must:

1. Describe the business in terms of the product or service that you are offering for sale.
2. Explain your methods for raising the capital to fund the business.
3. Describe the clientele that you are attempting to reach and why your business appeals to them.
4. Indicate your strategy for marketing your business.
5. Provide details on your business's potential for success and your methods for accomplishing that success.
6. Explain the government policies that may impact the establishment of this business (e.g., laws pertaining to anti-trust, fair trade, monopolies).

You must:

1. Present this project in class and attempt to persuade the class that your business could actually succeed.
2. Be prepared to answer questions from your classmates.
3. Participate in a class discussion on whether each business can be successful.
4. Vote for one business to win the title "most likely to succeed."

The creator of the winning project receives a prize.

RUBRIC: ECONOMICS PROJECT I—OPEN FOR BUSINESS

Name _____

Grade _____

1. The business plan (70 points)_____
   A. Has a name for the business (10 points)_____
   B. Completely describes the business (10 points) _____
   C. Clearly explains the methods for raising the capital (10 points)_____
   D. Defines the clientele and why the business appeals to them (10 points)_____
      _____
   E. Provides a clear marketing method (10 points)_____
   F. Explains the business's potential for success (10 points)_____
   G. Describes how to achieve success (10 points)_____
2. The presentation (30 points)_____
   A. Fully explains the business (10 points) _____
   B. Speaks persuasively (10 points)_____
   C. Engages the audience (10 points) _____

OVERVIEW: ECONOMICS PROJECT II—BUY THIS PRODUCT (MARKETING)

Project Type: Culminating; Independent

Objectives: To apply students' knowledge of marketing to creating advertising, students must:

1. Develop a prototype of a product or service.
2. Compose a plan for marketing the product or service.
3. Assemble demographic information about the target audience.
4. Produce a television or radio commercial.
5. Assess the impact that marketing has on demand.

Description: This project requires students to create and produce an original television or radio commercial to market the businesses they developed in project I.

Procedure: The teacher instructs the students to retrieve the business plans that they wrote for project I. The marketing ideas in these business plans serve as guidelines to develop a commercial for the product or service offered in the business plan.

1. First, the students review the marketing ideas that were included in the business plan.
2. Next, the students develop a prototype of the product or service created in project I.
3. Then the students compose demographic information such as age, gender, income, and education level for the target clientele.
4. Students then collate the demographic information with the marketing plan to develop a television or radio commercial for the business. Television commercials must be recorded on DVD and radio commercials must be recorded on CD.
5. The students present their commercials in class.
6. The class discusses each commercial's effectiveness in terms of its potential impact on demand.
7. The teacher awards first, second, and third place prizes for the best commercials, as determined by class vote.

HANDOUT: ECONOMICS PROJECT II—BUY THIS PRODUCT

Using the business plan that you created for project I, you must develop and produce a television or radio commercial that markets the product or service that your business plan offers. The commercial may not exceed sixty seconds in length.

1. Create a prototype of the product or service. It need not actually work, but the product must be original.
2. In writing, describe the demographic group you want to reach. Include your prospective clients' gender, typical age, educational level, income, and region of the country. This becomes part of your grade for this project.
3. Combine your demographic information with the marketing ideas proposed in your business plan, to design a persuasive commercial for your business.
4. Produce a radio or television commercial to promote this product. Be sure the commercial targets your demographic group. Television commercials must be recorded on DVD and radio commercials must be recorded on CD.
5. Include the prototype of your product in the commercial.
6. The prototype and the commercial must be presented in class.

First, second, and third place prizes are awarded for the best commercials.

RUBRIC: ECONOMICS PROJECT II—BUY THIS PRODUCT

Name _____

Grade _____

1. Demographic information is fully described (10 points) _____
2. The commercial represents the business that was designed in Project I (10 points)_____
   _____
3. The commercial clearly targets the intended market (10 points)_____
4. The marketing adheres to the original business plan (10 points)_____
5. The prototype is displayed in the commercial (10 points)_____
6. The prototype is original and is presented in class (10 points) _____
7. The commercial fully explains the product or service (10 points)_____
8. The commercial would increase demand (is persuasive) (10 points) _____
9. The commercial is in the correct format (DVD or CD) (10 points) _____
10. The commercial does not exceed sixty seconds in length (10 points)_____

OVERVIEW: ECONOMICS PROJECT III—LIVING AN ADULT LIFE (RUNNING A HOUSEHOLD)

Project Type: Culminating; Group

Objectives: To use students' knowledge of consumerism and budgeting in a "real-life" application, students must:

1. Search for a job online.
2. Develop a household budget with a partner.
3. Collaborate with a partner to establish and pay expenses for a household.
4. Write a paper detailing the creation of the household.

Description: In this project, students work as married couples or roommates to take on adult financial responsibilities. The student pairs then collaborate on developing a detailed paper (including illustrations) depicting their household and its budget.

Procedure: This project requires a great deal of online work. Therefore, the students conduct most of the online searches during several class periods. They then compose the paper and collect the photos and illustrations on their own time.

1. The teacher writes each boy's name on a small piece of paper.
2. Each girl in the class draws a boy's name. The boy then becomes her "husband" for the duration of the project. If the number of boys and girls is not equal, the remaining students may be paired as roommates. They must keep the same partner for the duration of the project.
3. During the first class period of research, each couple searches for jobs at websites such as www.monster.com or www.careerbuilder.com. They must select a job and print out the job posting. The couple must include these job postings in their project.
4. On their own time, the couples combine their salaries (as indicated in the job postings) to create a monthly budget.
5. During the next class period of research, the couples determine what town or city they want to live in. Then they search for a house or apartment in that city or town, using websites such as www.coldwellbanker.com or www.apartments.com, or any other pertinent website.
6. In subsequent class periods, the couples do online searches for furniture, groceries, clothing, and cars or alternate transportation. The couples may find appropriate websites for each of these categories of items by searching www.google.com. In each search, the couples must formulate itemized lists of their purchases, accompanied by illustrations (photos, drawings) of these purchases.
7. The couples must also include utilities and income taxes in their budget.
8. The couples collate the information they gathered into a detailed paper, along with the illustrations.
9. Each couple must present their household details to the class.

Differentiation: For special education classes, teachers may want to simplify this project by omitting step seven.

HANDOUT: ECONOMICS PROJECT III—LIVING AN ADULT LIFE

This project uses your knowledge of economics by requiring you to simulate adult financial responsibilities. The project also requires occasional work on the project in the computer lab where you may conduct your online searches. The remainder of the work must be completed at home.

1. You must have a partner to whom you are "married" or with whom you are roommates for the duration of this project. You may not divorce or separate during this project!
2. The two of you individually find jobs online. You must print out the job posting and include it in your project.
3. Then you and your spouse or roommate work together to create a monthly budget based on your combined salaries. The budget must include the following expenses: a house or apartment, a car or alternate transportation, groceries, furniture, clothing, utilities, and income taxes. You may include extraneous expenses such as vacations or other special purchases.
4. You then search online together to find all items listed in your budget. Be sure to record each item's price and to produce photos or drawings of each item.
5. Then you collate the information that you have gathered into a project. The project must include a paper that describes every aspect of your household budget. Be sure to include copies of all the information that you obtained online, as well as your monthly income and budget, with all expenses clearly indicated. Remember to include the photos or drawings of the items in your budget.
6. You must present and explain your household in class.

RUBRIC: ECONOMICS PROJECT III—LIVING AN ADULT LIFE

Name _____

Grade _____

1. The paper (80 points) _____
   A. Both students have indicated jobs (10 points)_____
   B. The monthly budget is based upon combined salaries (10 points)_____
   C. An affordable home is included (10 points)_____
   D. An affordable car or alternate transportation is included (10 points)_____
   E. Affordable furniture is included (10 points)_____
   F. A month's groceries are included (10 points)_____
   G. The cost of utilities is indicated (10 points)_____
   H. Income taxes are indicated (10 points)_____
   I. Photos or drawings of all budgeted items are included (10 points)_____
2. Oral presentation (10 points) _____
   A. The paper and illustrations are fully explained (5 points)_____
   B. Speaks with interest (5 points) _____

6

Psychology

Psychology is an elective course, which typically means that, unlike required courses, all students in the class have a genuine interest in the subject matter. That built-in attraction to the course makes it incumbent upon the teacher to maintain the students' attention, which is where activities and projects come in.

For the regular psychology course, which is taught in one semester, the teacher has a great deal of leeway in determining which topics are given greater attention and which are given little consideration. Therefore, the teacher has numerous opportunities for inserting activities into lessons. However, for the advanced placement psychology course, which usually is taught over the course of an entire school year, the teacher's freedom of choice in topics is virtually nonexistent. This teacher must be equitable in focusing on all areas in order to prepare his or her students to take the advanced placement exam. The result is that there is less time available for activities in the advanced placement course.

With these differences in mind, the activities in this chapter are well-suited to both levels of psychology courses. They are intended to activate the students' curiosity while building on existing knowledge acquired through the coursework and everyday experiences. Since these activities are accessible to all ability levels, no methods for differentiation are indicated for the activities in this chapter.

The projects, on the other hand, while within reach of both course levels, are designed with advanced placement students in mind, as these projects require the students to be more analytical, with an emphasis on synthesis and evaluation. However, differentiating these projects for regular psychology classes (or for special education students enrolled in regular classes) is simply a matter of omitting portions as the teacher sees fit. Some suggestions for differentiation are included for regular education classes and are suitable for special education students as well. Of course, the Individual Education Plan (IEP) for a special education student who enrolls in this course provides any additional modifications needed.

All projects in this chapter are designed to encourage each student's autonomous effort. With this chapter's emphasis on the students' analyses and evaluations, working independently puts the spotlight on these skills.

OVERVIEW: PSYCHOLOGY ACTIVITY I—CAFETERIA LIFE (BEHAVIORAL OBSERVATIONS)

Activity Type: Building; Independent

Objectives: To develop students' behavioral observation skills in a naturalistic setting, students must:

1. Observe behaviors.
2. List behaviors that are observed.
3. Categorize the behaviors observed.
4. Compare and contrast the lists.

Materials: Paper and pen

Description: Although this activity involves a class discussion after the fact, the actual observations take place in the cafeteria, outside of the class period. Students have the opportunity to play the role of "observational psychologist," which encourages the students to apply skills that they often unwittingly use. The students also analyze, synthesize, and evaluate the behaviors that they observe.

Procedure: During the students' assigned lunch periods, they observe all behaviors (other than eating) that occur in the cafeteria. Students must:

1. List the behaviors observed.
2. Categorize the behaviors as positive, negative, or neutral.
3. Bring the lists to class and discuss their observations.
4. Compare and contrast the observations made by students from the same lunch period as well as the observations made by students from different lunch periods.
5. Judge the categorization and characterization of the behaviors.
6. Draw conclusions about the process of naturalistic observation.

OVERVIEW: PSYCHOLOGY ACTIVITY II—HOP TO IT! (CLASSICAL CONDITIONING)

Activity Type: Motivating; Group

Objectives: To develop students' comprehension and assessment of classical conditioning, students must conduct an experiment in which they:

1. Predict outcomes.
2. Measure pulse rates.
3. Appraise results.
4. Draw conclusions.

Materials: Enough rope to make jump ropes for half of the students in the class, a stopwatch or a clock with a second hand, paper, and pens

Description: In this activity, students experience classical conditioning by participating in an experiment. As the experiment progresses, the students predict the expected result (hypothesize), evaluate their predictions' accuracy, and draw conclusions about the actual results.

Procedure: Students work in pairs to conduct an experiment in which one student plays the role of experimenter and the other is the participant.

1. The participant counts his or her pulse for sixty seconds as the experimenter keeps track of time.
2. The experimenter writes down the participant's pulse rate, which is recorded as the "resting rate."
3. The experimenter hands the participant a rope and instructs the participant to jump rope until told to stop.
4. The participant then jumps for thirty seconds as the experimenter keeps track of time.
5. The experimenter then retrieves the rope and repeats step one.
6. The pulse should be considerably higher, and is recorded by the experimenter as the "active rate."
7. Repeat the entire process two more times, making sure that the experimenter retrieves the rope after each period of jumping.
8. Allow the participant to relax for several minutes, until his or her pulse returns to the resting rate. During this period, the experimenters and participants discuss the reasons for the increased pulse rate that occurred after jumping, make predictions about the pulse rate they expect to have after relaxation, and explain the reasons for the predictions.
9. Repeat steps one and two.
10. The experimenter once again hands the participant the rope, but instead of asking the participant to jump, then directs the participant to check his or her pulse for thirty seconds.
11. The experimenter writes down the participant's pulse rate, which should be higher than the resting rate, yet lower than the active rate. This indicates that classical conditioning has occurred.
12. The class then draws conclusions about the reason for the results, and discusses whether the results coincided with predictions.

OVERVIEW: PSYCHOLOGY ACTIVITY III—SENSE ISN'T ALWAYS COMMON (SENSATION AND PERCEPTION)

Activity Type: Building; Independent

Objectives: To link sensation and perception with students' experience of the five senses, students must:

1. Distinguish between sensation and perception.
2. Identify specific sensations.
3. Determine the type of sensation being experienced.
4. Discover the interdependence of sensations.
5. Evaluate the differences in people's perceptions of the same sensation.
6. Discern the connections among sensation, perception, memory, and emotion.

Materials: Fabric to be used as a blindfold, paper napkins, and various items as follows: for gustatory sensation, salt and sugar; for olfactory sensation, a lemon, garlic, and cinnamon; for tactile sensation, saltine crackers, grapes, and cotton balls; for auditory sensation, various musical genres

Description: This activity has several experiments, each of which highlights one sensation. The teacher may prefer to choose only one experiment or may conduct all experiments over several class periods. During the experiments, students often rely on their perceptions of the other four sensations to interpret the sensation that is being studied.

Procedure: In each of the experiments in this activity, the teacher is in the role of experimenter and all students are participants.

For the gustatory sensation:

1. After distributing a paper napkin to each student, the teacher directs the students to close their eyes.
2. The teacher then pours small amounts of salt and sugar on each napkin.
3. Students then open their eyes and use sight, smell, and touch to distinguish between salt and sugar and to conclude which is which.
4. Students taste both items to determine whether their conclusions were correct.
5. The class discusses how their perceptions influenced their conclusions.

For the olfactory sensation:

1. The teacher directs the students to close their eyes.
2. One at a time, the teacher briefly places a sliced lemon, a garlic clove, and cinnamon beneath each student's nose and asks them to identify the smells silently.
3. The class discusses their conclusions about the aromas and their emotional reactions to each.
4. Using the students' reactions to the scents, the teacher leads the students to discover the links among sensation, perception, and emotion.

For the tactile sensation:

1. After distributing a paper napkin to each student, the teacher directs the students to close their eyes and open their hands with the palms up.

2. One at a time, the teacher touches each student's palm with the edge of a saltine cracker, a wet grape, and a cotton ball, leaving the three items on each napkin.
3. The teacher directs the students to keep their eyes closed and try to find and identify the items on the napkins.
4. The class discusses the difference in their ability to identify the items when they were touched with them (passive touch) as opposed to when they touched the items themselves, which is active touch.

For auditory sensation:

1. The teacher plays portions of songs from various cultures (such as Chinese, Latin, African) to demonstrate the high and low pitches of the auditory property known as frequency.
2. The teacher raises and lowers the volume to demonstrate the auditory property known as amplitude.
3. The teacher plays music featuring bands or orchestras to demonstrate the combination of instruments that is an example of the auditory property known as complexity.
4. Students express their reactions to the music as each song is played.
5. Students note and discuss the fact that the same sensation (in this case, auditory) produces different—often opposing—perceptions (interpretations and reactions).

For visual sensation:

1. The teacher directs the students to stand at the front of the classroom.
2. Working in pairs, one student in each pair is blindfolded.
3. After all obstacles have been removed from the floor, the blindfolded students are guided by their partners' verbal directions to find their way back to their seats.
4. In the absence of visual sensation, the blindfolded students must rely primarily on their sense of hearing, using the "cocktail-party effect" to distinguish the partner's voice from all others. The blindfolded students may also use touch to navigate the room without bumping into each other or the furniture.
5. The students in each pair then switch roles.
6. Students begin to realize that sensations are interdependent, particularly when one sense is not available.

OVERVIEW: PSYCHOLOGY ACTIVITY IV—WHAT PEOPLE DON'T KNOW ABOUT ME (DEVELOPMENT AND IDENTITY)

Activity Type: Motivating or Building; Group

Objectives: To explore the links among various aspects of psychology, including emotions, personality, memory, development, identity, and self-concept, students must:

1. Appraise themselves.
2. Categorize their own characteristics.
3. Recall past events.
4. Compare responses.

Materials: Paper and pen

Description: Working at the application level of Bloom's taxonomy, students apply their knowledge of psychology to assess themselves and to respond to questions about themselves. This activity can be used with any cognitive (as opposed to behavioral) aspect of psychology whenever a demonstration is needed. The teacher can easily adapt the activity to the topic being studied since the teacher determines which questions the students must ask each other. As such, the activity serves two purposes: self-examination and self-revelation.

Procedure: Students do this activity in pairs, repeating the process three times, with a different partner each time.

1. The teacher writes various "I" statements, such as "I'm good at . . . ," "I value . . . ," I wish . . . ," and "I don't think you know that I . . ." on the board.
2. The teacher also writes all class members' names on the board, leaving space next to each name.
3. The teacher directs students to select a partner.
4. One student in each pair is the interviewer and asks his or her partner to respond to the questions on the board. The interviewer takes notes about the responses. The students then reverse the roles.
5. The teacher keeps track of the time, allotting three minutes for each student to respond to the questions.
6. After this process has been done three times, with a different partner each time, the teacher then returns to the names listed on the board.
7. The teacher asks each student what they learned about the other students, and the teacher writes the responses beside their names.
8. The class compares and contrasts the responses.
9. The students identify and categorize the areas of psychology represented in this activity, and analyze how those areas are interconnected.

OVERVIEW: PSYCHOLOGY PROJECT I—ART IMITATES LIFE (PSYCHOLOGICAL PERSPECTIVES)

Project Type: Building; Independent

Objectives: To apply students' knowledge and comprehension of psychological perspectives in analyzing a work of nonfiction, students must:

1. Identify psychological concepts.
2. Specify the psychological problems presented in the book.
3. Define three psychological perspectives.
4. Apply the psychological perspectives to the book.

Description: In this project, students are introduced to psychological issues outside of the textbook's context. The project requires students to use the rudimentary knowledge that has been acquired in the first quarter of the school year as a basis for identifying and analyzing psychological concepts as they are presented in a work of psychological nonfiction.

Procedure: Students select a book from a recommended reading list provided by the teacher or, with the approval of the teacher, choose another book with a psychological emphasis. Each student writes a paper that:

1. Summarizes the book.
2. Identifies the psychological concepts presented in the book.
3. Describes the psychological problems presented in the book.
4. Defines and explains three psychological perspectives.
5. Applies the three psychological perspectives to address the problems in the book.
6. Critiques the book.

Differentiation: To modify this project for regular psychology classes, you may wish to omit steps four and five.

HANDOUT: PSYCHOLOGY PROJECT I—ART IMITATES LIFE

From the attached reading list, select a work of nonfiction that pertains to psychology and is interesting to you. You may choose a book on your own, with the teacher's approval. Write a paper that:

1. Summarizes the book.
2. Describes all psychological aspects presented in the book.
3. Defines three different psychological perspectives.
4. Explains the manner in which each perspective would seek to resolve the main issues presented in the book.
5. Critiques the issues and the manner in which they are presented.

The paper must be a minimum of _____pages, _____-spaced. The font must be size _____, type_____. Internal documentation is essential. Of course, there must be a cover page and a works cited page. In addition to the book that you choose, you must have two other sources (not including your textbook).

You must present the paper in class.

Suggested Reading List

Angry Men, Passive Men, Marvin Allen, Random House Publishing Group, ISBN-13: 9780449908112

Art, Mind and Brain: A Cognitive Approach to Creativity, Howard Gardner, Basic Books, ISBN-13:9780465004454

The Beauty Myth: How Images of Beauty Are Used against Women, Naomi Wolf, Harper Collins Publishers, ISBN-13: 9780060512187

Beyond Freedom and Dignity, B. F. Skinner, Hackett Publishing Company, Inc., ISBN-13: 9780872206274

A Child Called "It": One Child's Courage to Survive, David Pelzer, Health Communications, Inc., ISBN-13: 9781558742663

Choice Theory: A New Psychology of Personal Freedom, William Glasser, Harper Collins Publishers, ISBN-13: 9780060930141

Dibs in Search of Self: Story of an Emotionally Lost Child Who Found His Way Back, Virginia M. Axline, Random House Publishing, ISBN-13: 9780345339256

Emotional Intelligence, Daniel Goleman, Bantam Books, ISBN-13: 9780553383713

Flow: The Psychology of Optimal Experience, Mihaly Csikszentmihalyi, Harper Collins Publishers, ISBN-13: 9780060920432

Girl Interrupted, Susanna Kaysen, Random House, ISBN-13: 9780679746041

Hear These Voices: Youth at the Edge of the Millennium, Anthony Allison, Penguin Group (U.S.), Inc., ISBN-13: 9780525453536

Influence: The Psychology of Persuasion, Robert B. Cialdini, Harper Collins Publishers, ISBN-13: 9780061241895

The Lost Boy: A Foster Child's Search for the Love of a Family, David Pelzer, Health Communications, Inc., ISBN-13: 9781558745155

Love's Executioner and Other Tales of Psychotherapy, Irvin D. Yalom, Harper Collins Publishers, ISBN-13: 9780060958343

A Man Named Dave, David Pelzer, Penguin Group, ISBN-13: 9780452281905

The Man Who Tasted Shapes, Richard E. Cytowic, MIT Press, ISBN-13: 9780262532556

Me Talk Pretty One Day, David Sedaris, Little, Brown and Company, ISBN-13: 9780316776967

The Moral Animal: Why We Are the Way We Are: The New Science of Evolutionary Psychology, Robert Wright, Random House, Inc., ISBN-13: 9780679763994

My Year Off, Robert McCrum, Norton, W. W. & Company, Inc., ISBN-13: 9780393046564

Nobody's Child, Marie Balter and Richard Katz, Da Capo Press, ISBN-13: 9780201608168

One Child, Torey L. Hayden, Harper Collins Publishers, ISBN13: 9780380542628

The Social and Emotional Development of Gifted Children: What Do We Know? Maureen Neihart, Prufrock Press, ISBN-13: 9781882664771

Stumbling on Happiness, Daniel Gilbert, Knopf Publishing Group, ISBN-13: 9781400077427

There's a Boy in Here, Judy Barron and Sean Barron, Future Horizons, Inc., ISBN-13: 9781885477866

The Tiger's Child, Torey L. Hayden, Harper Collins Publishers, ISBN-13: 9780380725441

Twitch and Shout: A Touretter's Tale, Lowell Handler, University of Minnesota Press, ISBN-13: 9780816644513

What Should I Do with My Life? Po Bronson, Random House Publishing, ISBN-13: 9780345485922

Who Moved My Cheese? An Amazing Way to Deal with Change in Your Work and in Your Life, Spencer Johnson, Penguin Group, ISBN-13:9780399144462

RUBRIC: PSYCHOLOGY PROJECT I—ART IMITATES LIFE

Name _____

Grade _____

Scale: Excellent=5; Very Good=4; Good=3; Fair=2; Poor=1; Not Done=0

1. The paper's format (25 points)_____
   A. Font is size _____, type is_____ (5 points) _____
   B. Internal documentation is complete and accurate (5 points) _____
   C. Works cited page is complete (5 points) _____
   D. Cover page is included (5 points) _____
   E. Paper is minimum of _____ pages, _____-spaced_____ (5 points)_____
2. The paper's content (60 points)_____
   A. Contains complete, clearly explained summary (5 points)_____
   B. Fully describes *all* psychological aspects of book (5 points)_____
   C. Includes three psychological perspectives (5 points)_____
   D. Each perspective is accurately and fully defined (5 points)_____
   E. Fully explains how each perspective would seek to resolve the issue (5 points)_____
   F. Includes detailed personal analysis and opinion of the issue or book (5 points) _____
3. Presentation (15 points)_____
   A. Speaks clearly (5 points)_____
   B. Shows understanding of concepts presented (5 points)_____
   C. Shows enthusiasm_____

OVERVIEW: PSYCHOLOGY PROJECT II—A SELF-PORTRAIT (SELF-ANALYSIS)

Project Type: Culminating; Independent

Objectives: To apply students' knowledge of psychology to examining and evaluating themselves, students must:

1. Identify and describe the psychological theories with which they agree.
2. Identify and explain the psychological perspectives that they would use.
3. Analyze themselves in terms of specific psychological topics.
4. Hypothesize about their future lives.
5. Organize a particularly important aspect of their lives into one complete section of the project.

Description: This project requires the students to do somewhat of a psychological inventory of themselves. The self-assessment is presented in a book format that is divided into six sections, representing a compilation of words, photos, and any other creativity that the students wish to express within the defined parameters.

Procedure: Students purchase a large scrapbook or photo album in which they assemble the following information:

1. The psychological theorists and theories with whom they agree, along with the reasons for agreement.
2. The psychological perspectives that they would use as a psychologist and the reasons for their selection.
3. Self-analysis in terms of development, personality, intellect, emotion, and cognition.
4. A section each for their likes and dislikes.
5. A section for their hopes and expectations for their lives ten years from now.
6. A section that represents an important aspect of their lives.

Differentiation: For a regular psychology course, the teacher may prefer to omit steps one and two. Doing so would eliminate the discussion of psychological theories and perspectives, thereby placing a greater emphasis on the individual student's life.

HANDOUT: PSYCHOLOGY PROJECT II—A SELF-PORTRAIT

In a photo album, create a "portrait" of yourself using various words, pictures, photos, and lyrics that describe you. The portrait must contain the following six sections (and each section must be a minimum of six pages):

1. Section 1: This section includes a description or definition of the psychological theories and perspectives with which you agree and that you would use as a psychologist, as well as your reasons for choosing these perspectives and theories. This includes overall psychological perspectives as well as those relating to cognition, memory, intellect, development, emotion, and personality. A minimum of five is required.
2. Section 2: Entitled "I Am," this section contains a complete description of your personality traits, including your "color," developmental stage, cognitive stage, and intelligence style. In addition, there must be a large variety of everything that describes who you are (for example, athlete, daughter, friend, cheerful, studious) in both pictures and words.
3. Section 3: Entitled "I Like," this section includes exactly what the title indicates (in its entirety!). This should include many different pictures, photos, words, lyrics, poetry, or other items you consider relevant. Creativity and effort count.
4. Section 4: Entitled "I Dislike," like the preceding section, the title is self-explanatory. The only thing that you may not include is anyone's name. Once again, be creative!
5. Section 5: Entitled "My Life In Ten Years," this section describes your hopes and expectations for your life ten years from now, including profession, marital status, education level, residence, and anything else that may be part of your future life. Give a full and complete description. Use pictures from magazines or drawings to accompany the descriptions.
6. Section 6: You must design this section yourself. It may be entitled anything you want and may represent any aspect of you or your life. It must be at least _____ pages, creative, and interesting.

RUBRIC: PSYCHOLOGY PROJECT II—A SELF-PORTRAIT

Name _____

Grade _____

Section One: (20 points) _____

    1. Contains a minimum of five perspectives/theories (5 points)_____

    2. Theories are explained (10 points)_____

    3. Reasons for selecting the theories are given (5 points)_____

Section Two: (20 points) _____

    1. Personality traits/color are included (5 points)_____

    2. Stages of life are included (10 points)_____

    3. Various aspects of "who you are" are included (5 points)_____

Section Three: (10 points) _____

    1. Includes many different "likes" (5 points)_____

    2. Shows effort and creativity (5 points)_____

Section Four: (10 points) _____

    1. Includes various "dislikes" (5 points)_____

    2. Shows effort and creativity (5 points)_____

Section Five: (15 points) _____

    1. Fully describes future life (7 points)_____

    2. Includes pictures or drawings (8 points)_____

Section Six: (15 points) _____

    1. Represents your life (5 points)_____

    2. Is a minimum of _____ pages (5 points)_____

    3. Shows effort and creativity (5 points)_____

Presentation (10 points) _____

    1. Speaks clearly (5 points)_____

    2. Speaks with enthusiasm/interest (5 points)_____

OVERVIEW: PSYCHOLOGY PROJECT III—THE DOCTOR IS IN (PSYCHOLOGICAL ANALYSIS)

Project Type: Culminating; Independent

Objectives: To synthesize all psychological concepts learned by the students throughout the course, students must completely analyze another person, including:

1. Researching a person's life.
2. Summarizing the person's life.
3. Analyzing the person's development.
4. Identifying and describing the psychological issues and/or problems.
5. Prescribing appropriate treatment for the issues and problems presented.

Description: This project represents the culmination of the course. Beginning at the lowest level of Bloom's taxonomy and progressing to the highest level, students incorporate all concepts learned throughout the course. The students apply these concepts to the analysis of a person, based on information obtained via a biography and biographical research on the Internet.

Procedure: The teacher assigns each student to research the life of anyone the student considers interesting and to read a biography of this person. Then each student, in the role of psychologist, writes a paper that:

1. Summarizes the person's life.
2. Completely psychologically analyzes the person.
3. Identifies and describes the psychological issues or problems presented in the biography.
4. Prescribes and explains appropriate treatment for these psychological problems or issues.

Differentiation: For the regular psychology course, the teacher may prefer to completely alter this project by requiring that the students do only steps one and two. With this type of modification, the students would still need to analyze the person studied, but without the original project's depth.

HANDOUT: PSYCHOLOGY PROJECT III—THE DOCTOR IS IN

Read a biography or autobiography of any person who interests you (for example, a politician, entertainer, athlete, or historic person) and complete the following:

1. Summarize the person's life.
2. Using developmental psychology, explain the impacts on this person's development in childhood, adolescence, and adulthood.
3. Describe two different personality theories that explain this person's behavior.
4. Analyze cognition, memory, sensation and perception, motivation, emotion, and intelligence as they relate to this person.
5. Based on your knowledge of psychology, analyze this person's behavior in terms of whether he or she has a psychological disorder (if so, explain). Whether you conclude that the person has a disorder or not, you must also consider whether the person has behaviors that cause or contribute to the difficulties he or she encounters in life (if so, describe them).
6. Suggest at least two therapies that would help this person.
7. The paper must be a minimum of _____ pages, _____-spaced, size ___, font, _____, with internal documentation. A cover page and a works cited page must also be included.
8. Turn in a copy of the paper in class.
9. Present the paper in class.

RUBRIC: PSYCHOLOGY PROJECT III—THE DOCTOR IS IN

Name _____

Grade _____

1. The paper's format (25 points) _____
   A. Cover page is included (5 points) _____
   B. Font is size ____, type is _____ (5 points) _____
   C. Paper is _____pages, _____-spaced (5 points) _____
   D. Internal documentation is correct and complete (5 points) _____
   E. Works cited page is correct and complete (5 points) _____
2. The paper's content (60 points) _____
   A. Person's entire life is summarized (5 points) _____
   B. Person's entire development is analyzed (5 points) _____
   C. Two different personality theories are used (5 points) _____
   D. Cognition, memory, sensation/perception, motivation, emotion, and intelligence are evaluated (5 points)
   _____
   E. Psychological disorders are analyzed (5 points) _____
   F. Two therapies are suggested (5 points) _____
3. Presentation (15 points) _____
   A. Clearly explains the person presented (5 points) _____
   B. Shows knowledge of relevant psychological concepts (5 points) _____
   C. Speaks clearly and with interest (5 points) _____

7

Sociology

Sociology is an elective course. Taught in one semester, it's usually open to high school students of all grade levels. This challenges the teacher to simultaneously reach all grade levels and still keep the students engaged. With that in mind, this chapter has an eclectic mix of interactive activities and projects designed to provoke thought and foster new perceptions of old situations.

As a behavioral science, sociology has much in common with psychology. This is why the activities in this chapter can easily be adapted to a psychology course and vice versa. Unlike the psychology course, however, sociology does not have an advanced placement or honors level. Without a test for which to prepare the students, the teacher has a good deal of latitude in determining which topics become central to the course. In fact, this class can be conducted much like a college course, with the teacher concentrating solely on those topics that he or she considers most salient or those in which the students seem to be most interested.

Therefore, all the assignments in this chapter reflect topics that often provoke student interest and discussion. To begin that discussion, the activities are in the motivating category, as each is also intended to introduce a new lesson. The projects, of course, emphasize societal issues—from what defines a perfect society to the concerns that confront today's society.

Like the previous chapter, these activities require no differentiation, as they are designed for all ability levels. Similarly, only one project (project II) needs tips for differentiation, which are included.

OVERVIEW: SOCIOLOGY ACTIVITY I—WHICH IS BETTER? (PREJUDICE)

Activity Type: Motivating; Group

Objectives: To discover the basis for prejudice, students must:

1. Examine objects.
2. Compare and contrast the objects.
3. Appraise the objects' values.
4. Ascertain whether their appraisals were correct.
5. Explain and assess the basis for their appraisals.

Materials: small, gift-wrapped packages

Description: This activity is designed to provide a tangible example of prejudice. In small groups, the students select the "best" gift from a pile and then discover whether their assessment was correct. This discovery becomes the basis for a class discussion on how prejudices are formed.

Procedure: The teacher gift-wraps several small packages in different kinds of wrapping paper, so that none is alike.

1. The teacher places the packages on a table in the classroom before the students arrive.
2. The teacher asks the students which package is best.
3. Then the teacher allows randomly selected students to select the best package from the table.
4. After all packages have been removed from the table, the students open the packages and discover that, in fact, no package is better than the others because all are empty.
5. The teacher leads a discussion of their methods for determining which package was best. This is likely to elicit responses that refer to the manner in which the package was wrapped, or their preference for a particular color, or conjecture regarding the contents of the package.
6. The teacher explains that their methods for selecting the packages were based on prejudice (prejudging) and then begins a lesson on prejudice in society.

OVERVIEW: SOCIOLOGY ACTIVITY II—HOW DO I LOOK? (UNIVERSALITY OF EMOTION)

Activity Type: Motivating; Group

Objectives: To discover the universal manner in which human emotions are expressed and perceived in all societies, students must:

1. Dramatize various emotions.
2. Identify emotions.
3. Determine the basis for identifying the emotions.
4. Discuss the commonalities of emotional expression throughout the world.

Materials: None

Description: In this activity, done in conjunction with a lesson on cultural mores, students are able to discover the universal manner in which the six basic human emotions are expressed and understood throughout the world.

Procedure: On separate pieces of paper, the teacher writes each of the six basic human emotions (anger, joy, sadness, surprise, fear, disgust) as well as any other emotions that the teacher chooses to include.

1. Student volunteers randomly select a paper.
2. The student then stands before the class and acts out the emotion indicated on the paper, without using words.
3. The class members guess the emotion that is being conveyed.
4. When all emotions have been dramatized, the teacher asks the students to explain which emotions were more difficult to discern and why. The six basic emotions surface as the ones that are more readily conveyed and perceived.
5. The teacher then teaches a lesson on the cross-cultural nature of facial expression regarding the six basic emotions.

OVERVIEW: SOCIOLOGY ACTIVITY III—WHEN THE UNEXPECTED OCCURS (COLLECTIVE BEHAVIOR)

Activity Type: Motivating; Group

Objectives: To illustrate the influences on group behavior, students must:

1. Participate in a social experiment.
2. Observe aberrant behavior.
3. Decide whether to go along with the aberrant behavior.
4. Explain their decision.
5. Discuss the impact of the witnessed behavior on their thought processes.

Materials: None

Description: Students who volunteer to act as confederates in this activity display rebellion in an attempt to influence their classmates' behavior. This activity is intended to be part of a lesson on collective behavior or can effectively be used in lessons on deviance or societal values.

Procedure: Prior to the start of class, the teacher selects one or two students who are perceived as leaders by the other students to be confederates (knowledgeable participants) in this activity.

1. The teacher instructs the confederates to behave in opposition to the tasks that the teacher assigns during the class period.
2. After beginning the lesson, the teacher assigns any labor-intensive task that must be completed within very limited time constraints. For example, students might write a detailed essay in ten minutes, or research a topic and prepare a presentation on it in a half hour. Any task that could not properly be completed in such a brief amount of time is effective.
3. The confederates immediately begin to complain loudly about the assignment, increasing in volume and anger as the teacher calmly refuses to change the assignment.
4. The confederates then demand to know if anyone else agrees with them.
5. If all goes well, at least one student should begin to speak in support of the confederates' argument.
6. Then the teacher reveals the experiment to the entire class and leads a discussion of why the students reacted as they did to the confederates' behavior. Possible reasons include precipitating factors, structural strain, and generalized belief.

OVERVIEW: SOCIOLOGY PROJECT I—WHAT A WONDERFUL WORLD (UTOPIAN SOCIETY)

Project Type: Culminating; Independent

Objectives: To develop a plan for a perfect society, students must:

1. Determine what a perfect society would be.
2. Develop a written plan for the society.
3. Specify and elaborate on their sociological perspective.
4. Define the society's norms, values, and mores.
5. Describe the society's culture.
6. Explain how the society would function.

Description: This project entails the students creating and expressing their ideas of a perfect society. It requires them to use sociological constructs to develop their societal plans in a book format.

Procedure: The teacher instructs the students to create their ideas of a perfect society and to develop it into an illustrated book.

1. First, each student must explain his or her sociological perspective.
2. Then, based on that perspective, each student must decide what a perfect society would be.
3. Next, the student formulates a plan for the society's creation and functioning. The plan must include the society's name, culture, norms, values, and mores.
4. The students must then fully develop the society in a book, with illustrations or photos of the homes, businesses, technology, transportation, vegetation, and anything else that reflects the society.
5. Each student must present his or her book in class.

HANDOUT: SOCIOLOGY PROJECT I—WHAT A WONDERFUL WORLD

Using your knowledge of sociology, design and develop a book that reflects and illustrates your ideas of the perfect society. In addition to using words, include pictures, drawings, photographs, or anything else that you consider suitable. In the book, you must:

1. Indicate and explain your sociological perspective.
2. Create a perfect society based on your sociological perspective. The society must:
   A. Have a name.
   B. Detail your society's culture, values, norms, and mores.
   C. Completely describe how your society functions.
   D. Explain (in sociological terms) why this is the ideal society.
   E. Include drawings or photos of the homes, businesses, technology, transportation, and vegetation of the society. Creativity counts.
3. You must present the book in class.

RUBRIC: SOCIOLOGY PROJECT I—WHAT A WONDERFUL WORLD

Name _____

Grade _____

1. The project is in a book format (10 points) _____

2. The society has a name (5 points)_____

3. The sociological perspective is indicated and explained (15 points) _____

4. The society's culture, norms, mores, and values are fully described (20 points)_____
_____

5. The society is completely described (20 points) _____

6. The society is fully functional (20 points)_____

7. The book is fully illustrated (10 points) _____

OVERVIEW: SOCIOLOGY PROJECT II—NOW HEAR THIS (PROPAGANDA)

Project Type: Culminating; Independent

Objectives: To assess propaganda's effect on societal beliefs and values, students must:

1. Research a major world event.
2. Analyze the factors that led to the event.
3. Evaluate the sociological influences on the event and the society.
4. Assess the roles of the media, event leaders, and the government in promoting a particular viewpoint (propaganda).
5. Infer a different outcome for the event, based on the removal of one outlet for the propaganda.
6. Compare and contrast all events as presented in class.

Description: This project assists students in assessing and judging the impact of propaganda and sociological factors on major events and vice versa. Students have completed the unit on society and values prior to this project.

Procedure: The teacher provides the students with a list of major events from which they may select.

1. Each student selects an event to research.
2. The research must include the precipitating factors, the societal influences, and the decisions made by the leaders.
3. The students review newspapers of the time to analyze the manner in which the media reported the information leading to the major event.
4. Then the students do the same in evaluating the information put forth by the governments or the other leaders involved in the event.
5. The students then collate the information into a research paper.
6. Then the students add their own assessment of the event and its surrounding factors, particularly the propaganda, from a sociological viewpoint. This must include sociological perspectives as well as relevant sociological terms and concepts.
7. The final aspect of the paper focuses on how the event might have been prevented or its outcome altered, by limiting or removing one of the outlets for the propaganda.
8. Each student presents the paper in class.
9. After all papers have been presented, the teacher leads a class discussion that compares and contrasts the role of propaganda in all events that were presented.

Differentiation: If sociology is taught to a special education classes, teachers of these classes may modify this project by limiting the choice of events as well as the number of variables to be considered in the research paper.

HANDOUT: SOCIOLOGY PROJECT II—NOW HEAR THIS

Many factors influence the occurrence of major world events. You will select an event from the list below and write a research paper. The paper must include the following:

1. The occurrences that led to the event.
2. The societal factors that influenced the event.
3. The decisions made by the event's leaders.
4. The manner in which the newspapers of the time reported on the factors leading to the event (and the event itself). Does this reflect propaganda?
5. The manner in which the event's leaders and the government presented the event to the participants and to the public. Does this reflect propaganda?
6. Your evaluation of the event and propaganda's impact on the event. This must be written from a sociological perspective, using sociological terms and concepts.
7. How the event might have been prevented or its outcome altered by limiting or removing one outlet for propaganda.
8. The research paper must be _____ pages long, with a font size _____, font type_____. Be sure to include internal documentation, a works cited page, and a cover page.

You must present your paper in class.

Major Events

Abolitionism

Afghanistan War

Civil rights movement

Genocide in Darfur, Sudan

The Great Depression

Gulf War (1991)

The Holocaust

Iran hostage crisis

Iraq War

Israeli-Palestinian conflicts

"Los Desaparecidos" in Argentina

Russian Revolution

Spanish-American War

Vietnam protest movement

Women's rights movement

Women's suffrage movement

World War I

World War II

RUBRIC: SOCIOLOGY PROJECT II—NOW HEAR THIS

Name _____

Grade _____

1. The paper's format (25 points) _____
    A. Font is size _____, font type is _____ (5 points) _____
    B. Internal documentation is correct and complete (5 points) _____
    C. Works cited page is correct and complete (5 points) _____
    D. Cover page is included (5 points) _____
    E. Paper is minimum of _____ pages, _____-spaced (5 points)_____
2. The paper's content (95 points) _____
    A. Explains the occurrences that led to the event (10 points)_____
    B. Describes the societal factors that influenced the event (10 points)_____
    C. Explains the decisions made by the leaders (10 points)_____
    D. Analyzes the media's role in reporting the events (10 points)_____
    E. Assesses the leaders' or government's version of the events (10 points)_____

    _____
    F. Fully evaluates the event and propaganda's impact on the event, using sociological terms, concepts, and per-
         spectives (15 points)_____
    G. Considers how limiting or removing a propaganda outlet would have affected the event and/or its outcome
         (10 points)_____

OVERVIEW: SOCIOLOGY PROJECT III—HOW WE LIVE (SURVEY ON A SOCIOLOGICAL TOPIC)

Project Type: Culminating; Independent

Objectives: To assess students' ability to analyze and synthesize sociological issues through surveys, students must:

1. Study a current sociological issue.
2. Create a list of survey questions.
3. Survey a random sampling of people.
4. Analyze the responses to the survey.
5. Interpret the survey's statistical results.

Description: In this project, students formulate survey questions on a topical issue of their choosing and survey a random sampling of the target population.

Procedure: The teacher instructs the students to select a sociological issue that is interesting to them.

1. Each student first determines who the target population is for this issue.
2. Then each student formulates a list of at least twenty questions pertaining to the target population's experiences, habits, and/or opinions on this issue.
3. The students decide how to reach a random sample of the target population and then survey that sample.
4. Then the students review and analyze the survey's results.
5. Next, the students represent the results statistically.
6. The students then write a paper that describes the sociological issue that was studied, explains how the target population and the sample were chosen, and evaluates and interprets the survey's responses and statistics.
7. The students present the paper in class.
8. The teacher leads a discussion that compares and contrasts the studies' methodologies as well as the results.

HANDOUT: SOCIOLOGY PROJECT III—HOW WE LIVE

Many sociological issues affect today's society. Select one issue (such as crime, marriage, substance abuse, dating, college life) that is interesting to you and complete the following tasks:

1. Determine who the target population is in this issue.
2. Develop a list of at least twenty questions that you use to survey your target population.
3. Hypothesize (in writing) about the results you expect to obtain.
4. Decide how to find a random sample of the target population.
5. Survey the random sample.
6. Review the responses and represent them statistically in a graph or chart.
7. Write a paper that describes the sociological issue that you studied, explains who the target population is and how you selected a random sample, and analyzes and interprets the responses and the statistics.
8. Include your hypothesis and the list of questions that you used in your survey. Also indicate why the hypothesis was or was not correct.
9. Present the paper in class.

RUBRIC: SOCIOLOGY PROJECT III—HOW WE LIVE

Name _____

Grade _____

1. The chosen sociological issue is fully described (10 points) _____

2. The method for choosing a random sample of the target population is explained (10 points)_____

   _____

3. The responses to the survey are fully analyzed (20 points)_____

4. The responses are also represented statistically in a chart or graph (10 points)_____

   _____

5. The statistics are accurately interpreted (20 points) _____

6. The survey contains a minimum of twenty relevant questions (10 points) _____

   _____

7. The hypothesis is clearly explained (10 points) _____

8. The reasons that the hypothesis was correct (or not) are explained (10 points) _____

   _____

About the Author

Denise Fawcett Facey is an educator, public speaker, and workshop leader. The recipient of awards that include Inspirational Teacher and STAR Teacher, she holds a master's degree in education. She is a member of the Authors Guild and writes on educational and inspirational topics.